BIG LOUIE & ME

D1322172

BIG LOUIE & ME

Caravans, curses & cockfights

GEORGE LOCKE

University of Hertfordshire Press

First published in Great Britain in 2012 by
University of Hertfordshire Press
College Lane
Hatfield
Hertfordshire
AL10 9AB
UK

© George Locke 2012

The right of George Locke to be identified as the author
of this work has been asserted by him in accordance with
the Copyright, Designs and Patents Act 1988.

All rights reserved. No part of this book may be
reproduced or utilised in any form or by any means,
electronic or mechanical, including photocopying,
recording or by any information storage and retrieval
system, without permission in writing from the publisher.

British Library Cataloguing in Publication Data
A catalogue record for this book is available from the
British Library

ISBN 978-1-907396-82-3

Design by Arthouse Publishing Solutions Ltd
Printed in Great Britain by MPG Books Group Ltd

To my lovely wife Maggy, who is of
great goodness and long suffering

With a big thank you to Jo for her patience
in doing the computer work, all the typing,
re-typing, and re-re-typing, and without whose
help this book wouldn't have been finished

'I KNOW TOO well its truth, from experience, that whenever any poor Gypsies are encamped anywhere crimes and robberies occur it is invariably laid to their account, which is shocking, and if they are always looked upon as vagabonds how can they become good people? I trust in heaven that the day may come when I may do something for these poor people.'

> *Extract from the 1836 diary of Queen Victoria.*
> *Wise words for someone so young and in such an*
> *exalted position. Has anything changed?*

CONTENTS

1

BIG LOUIE

IN THE YEAR 1869 my great gran Alice, who was a *gorgio* (non-Gypsy), did a very silly thing. At the age of fourteen she ran away from home with one of the local Gypsy boys, Joe Locke, but as soon as he found out she was carrying a baby he disappeared. Alice went back to the village, where she gave birth to my Grandad. A couple of years later, now aged sixteen, she married a distant cousin of hers called Nathan Miller who was also a *gorgio*, moved to his farm in Worcestershire and had a lot more children.

Grandad told me that by the time he was eleven he could no longer put up with the cruelty meted out by his stepfather, so he packed his bags and went in search of his birth father, Joe Locke, whom he had never seen. He said he went to the nearest community of Gypsies and explained what he was doing. There were no Lockes on the camp but a few days later they took him to another Gypsy camp and left him there. Those Gypsies were also unable to help him find his dad but they took him to some more Gypsies who they thought might be able to help him. This happened many times but Grandad said they were all very kind to him and were anxious for him to find his Dad.

After being on the road for over nine months, he was crossing a field near Burton-on-Trent heading to another camp when he met a woman who, from the way she was dressed, seemed to be a Gypsy. She stared at him and they both stopped.

She kept on looking him up, then said, 'What's your name boy?'

He answered, 'Miller.'

Looking at him intently, she said, 'Are you sure your name isn't Locke? Because you look exactly like my man.'

She took him to the camp and called her husband, who was a big raw-boned man. He came across, looking at Grandad with puzzlement all over his face. The woman said nothing. With a mounting sense of excitement, Grandad asked the man if he was Joe Locke, to which he replied that he was. When Joe had heard the boy's story he pulled him to him and hugged him. Turning to his wife, he said, 'Mercy, this is my eldest son and we are going to look after him.' The woman also hugged Grandad and said, 'You'd better come and meet your brothers and sisters.'

He suddenly found out he had five brothers and four sisters, who immediately treated him as their eldest brother, and Joe and Mercy treated him as their eldest son. All the other Gypsies gathered round and were told the story of Grandad's travels and how proud Joe was that he had walked all that way to find him.

Grandad quickly settled to the Romany way of life. Although he was only eleven, he was used to working hard on his stepfather's farm and was always willing to help with seasonal work in the fields and any other tasks asked of him. He had a natural affinity with horses and had the knack of instinctively knowing what was causing a horse to be unwell. His dad grew very proud of him and at every opportunity praised him and never tired of telling anybody who would listen what a good eldest son he had. Surprisingly, Grandad's half-brothers and sisters never showed any jealousy and were genuinely pleased for him. It wasn't long before his stepmother forgot his origins and loved and treated him as her own.

Grandad told me that one of the most exciting times of his life was when, after sharing a *vardo* (wooden wagon) with his half-brothers for five years or so, his dad told him he was going to give him his own wagon and two horses on his sixteenth birthday when he became a man. His dad also told him it was about time he started looking for a wife.

At the age of seventeen Grandad met a full Romany called Louisa Smith (later known as Big Louie) at the horse fair at Stow-on-the-Wold. After a short courtship they decided to get married. The date was fixed and Gran – Louisa – told me that on the day there were about sixty to seventy horse-drawn wagons, all freshly painted in bright colours, with all the Tribes including Smiths, Lockes, Boswells, Bucklands, Burtons, Lees and many others dressed in their best traditional clothes. All the wagons except the Gypsy Queen's were down at one end of the field whilst the Queen's was separated from the rest and a screen had been put up in front so the assembled Gypsies couldn't see what went on behind it. Usually the Queen (also known as the *Krallissi* or the *Jinimengri* – Wise One) is one of the oldest women in the community with the ability to communicate well with the other women and advise them on birth, marriages, deaths, female customs and taboos. She also settles any disputes between the women. The Queen is a powerful woman within the Tribe and held in great respect – even by the men.

Grandad waited anxiously by the wagon for his bride and felt so proud when Gran came down the steps in all her finery followed by the Gypsy Queen – she is a very important person in the hierarchy of the Romanies and is responsible for conducting the wedding service. The Queen was carrying a large pewter pot all beautifully etched and decorated. The two women went behind the screen, out of sight from everyone else, where the Queen placed the pot on the ground and Gran stooped over it and weed into it. She then came out from behind the screen and Grandad took her place, picked up the pewter pot and also weed into it. Then he gave the pot to the Queen who, in front of all the Tribes, stood between my Gran and Grandad, swilkered the waters round and round and then said, 'Their marriage will last until these waters are separated!' Everyone watching the ceremony cheered, clapped and shouted; the celebration had begun. The music, dancing, singing, drinking and feasting went on into the early hours of the next morning.

Eleven months after their marriage along came my dad, Thomas, who was born when Gran was seventeen in 1887. By the time she was forty-five she had eighteen surviving children, ten girls and eight boys, with some very interesting names. After Thomas there was Noah, Mizella, Sinnaminti, John, Zacharia, Nathaniel, Isaac, Jacob, Sarah, George, Ezra, Chirri, Lavender, Ezrine, Adelaide, Asima and Reuben. Aunty Adelaide told me (although she didn't know when) that Gran had had at least three more children only they didn't survive. (Adelaide also told me that she had been named in memory of three family members, Shadrach, Esau and Simeon, who had been transported to Australia. Apparently only Shadrach came back and it was he who suggested her name.)

In later life Gran became very fat and although she was only four foot ten she weighed nearly eighteen stone. If she lay on her belly she was four foot ten, if she lay on her side she was four foot ten. No matter which way she was she was still four foot ten!

My first recollection of Gran dates from the very early 1940s when she was in her seventies. She always wore a man's peaked cap or sometimes a trilby, always on the side of her head, never on the top. She had smoked a pipe from the age of three. Apparently, every time her grandad packed his pipe, he would pack a small one he had fashioned for his granddaughter, light it, pop it into her mouth and she would sit there puffing away until all the tobacco had gone.

All she had was one tooth, her sharp-pointed eye tooth, which she called her 'pickle-onion tooth' because at the start of an evening she would wedge a pickle onion onto it and she could suck on that all night. Her dresses were long and voluminous and came right down to the ground. You couldn't see her feet but you could hear her coming because she always wore hob-nailed boots. She wore these for one reason and that was for kicking people when she was drunk, which was quite often. She loved stopping near a market town where they had an extended licence. If she got into the pubs early and had a really long session she could drink about twelve pints of stout.

There was many a time when my Mom, with her brood of seven children, was going through a village or town when suddenly Mom would say, 'Oh my God, there's your Gran coming out the pub. Quick!' She would drag us away before we were seen. Gran would be staggering about, drunk as a 'bobby owler', staggering all over the place, with her hat on the side of her head, her arms up in the air and fists clenched, shouting and bawling, 'Come on, who wants a fight? Man or 'ooman, don't be cowards, who's gonna take me on?' Should anyone approach her, she would have a go at them. We were in one village and saw the policeman coming down the lane; he saw Gran, turned round and went back the other way. The last time he had tried to arrest her it had been raining, he slipped over and Gran sat on him.

Romanies love colours, and Gran got a black straw hat from somewhere covered with multi-coloured flowers. She loved that hat. The day after she got it she put it on and went up the village to swank and show off her new hat. Picking up her shopping bag and putting on her hat, she went into the local store, filled her bag with groceries and left the shop to go back to the camp. Unfortunately, by this time it was raining so she stood under the shop's awning to wait for it to stop. It didn't, it came down faster and faster. She was being watched by five men – the two shopkeepers and three villagers who were standing across the other side of the square under another awning. After about twenty minutes Gran decided she must get back to cook some of the food, but she didn't want to get her lovely hat wet, so she caught hold of the hem of her dress and lifted it up behind her, eventually pulling her frock up over her hat. Then she bent down to get her groceries and one of the men across the square shouted, 'Oi Louie, we can see your backside.' To which Gran replied, 'I don't give a bugger. I've had this backside seventy-six years, I only had me hat yesterday!'

She was very well-known for her knowledge of medicines and if we stayed near a village or small town without its own hospital, doctors' surgery or chemist, it wouldn't be long before some of the villagers, adults as well as children, would call to see Gran and she would minister to them.

She made a variety of lotions, potions, salves and poultices, nearly all from plants growing in the hedgerow.

To say some of her 'cures' smelt distasteful would be to put it very mildly – some were absolutely rancid. For a mild pain she would introduce willow into her medicine; willow is *salix* in Latin and contains salicin, a substance that closely resembles aspirin. For an extreme pain, say a sprained ankle, she would anoint the painful area with a salve containing mandrake (bryony), aconite and belladonna (nightshade).

Another example of her medicine is when she would make a jam and, instead of using it, keep it until the contents had turned completely to mould. Should anyone have cut themselves, the mould would be rubbed into the wound and bound up – early penicillin. She didn't know it was that, but the Tribe had been doing it for many generations.

She was perhaps best known for her remedies to counteract colds, sore throats, coughs and earache – after you had been treated once you were too afraid to catch another cold!

In the early 1940s when I was little and occasionally went to school, there would be at least forty children in the class and if, in the depths of winter, one child got a cold you could more or less guarantee that almost the whole class would develop a cold. So there would be twenty-five to thirty children with snail trails up their sleeves and all with a lovely pair of 'snot-candles'. There were the earliest signs that something was amiss, then they would all develop a sore throat together with a hacking cough when every child sounded like a sea lion. As the cough subsided, everybody would suffer from earache, so it meant a visit to my Gran at each of these stages.

At the first stage of the cold your clothes were pulled up around your neck, you were forced to lie down and then you were covered in animal grease at least five years old. It smelt worse than anything else I've ever known, a cross between rotting flesh and a farm cesspool. After the grease had been put on, a piece of paper was laid on your chest while Gran fetched an iron which had been heating on the fire and this was used to iron you. Sometimes the iron was so hot it burnt your chest. Should you complain she smacked you across the mouth with her heavily ringed fingers and probably split your lip. You only complained once! When the ironing was finished the smelly grease would have melted and run everywhere, under your arms, down your belly, and all over your shirt and pullover. You were then unceremoniously kicked out and the next child would receive the same treatment.

So next morning twenty-five to thirty children, all covered with the horrible-smelling animal grease, would troop into the classroom and sit down. As it was winter time the radiators would be on full blast, making the room very hot. The ones who sat near the radiators started to smell first. When ten to fifteen minutes had gone by the whole classroom would reek of the repulsive fat. Despite the snow, all the windows would be opened, but even that didn't take the smell away. Having sat there for several days smelling dreadful, the sore throat and sea lion cough – known as croup – would start. This meant another visit to Big Louie.

Gran had bottles and bottles of syrup made from cabbage and pungent hedgerow herbs, which she claimed would cure sore throats and coughs. She would hand you some in a container, perhaps a tin can or a bottle, and urge you to drink it. The child being treated would smell it long before getting it to their mouth and usually said, 'I ain't taking that.' The syrup smelt just a little less horrible than the animal grease. It was as if somebody had cooked cabbage, drained it into a container and put the lid on, then, after a couple of weeks or so, opened it up again: if you can imagine the pungent odour that would emanate from that would be very much like the smell of this syrup. Gran would offer you the container once or twice again, then she'd say, 'This is the *last* time – *tek it!*'. And if you didn't, she'd put it down on the table and start moving towards you. Any child would want to run from her, but Gran had mesmerising eyes and once you looked at her – and nearly every girl or boy did – you couldn't move. You would finish up in a headlock with your little head pulled tight into her big fat side while she inched you towards the table. As you went, two of her great big banana fingers would be stuffed up your nose. With her fingers up your nose, you had to open your mouth to breathe, and no sooner was the mouth open then Gran would pick up the bottle, shove it into your mouth and pour a large quantity of syrup down your throat. Nearly every child got the same treatment as none of them would drink the stuff, it was so vile.

So next day in school there would be twenty-five to thirty children covered in disgusting smelly animal grease and now liberally dosed with cabbage syrup, which had an undesired side effect: it gave all the children flatulence, and as they sat on the hard seats they only had to move their little bums just a fraction and they would break wind. The room, already filled with the stench of the warm animal fat, was now ringing with a crescendo of purping. If we had had a music teacher we could have played the national anthem!

This continued for several days, then the children would start to get earache. Back to my Gran's where she had an everlasting stock of baked onions. She would stuff each ear with an onion core, then, to stop you taking them out, a bandage was tied round your head. The next day in school the children would still be covered in grease, all purping away and now they had onions in their ears. The teacher was wasting his time talking because they couldn't hear him.

Some of Louie's cures worked a bit too well sometimes. There was one ailment which was very prevalent back then: she would guarantee to cure it in twenty to thirty minutes maximum, but it was dire and very painful, and I always thought people were rather silly to take Gran's medicine to cure constipation! Depending on the severity of the condition, she would use the particular potion she thought was needed. A 'cure' could contain all or some of the following: blackthorn, garlic, wormwood, holly, buckthorn and black treacle. The strongest, for severe cases, could act nearly as quickly as an enema. She always advised that this should be taken at home and not to venture too far for a while!

When I was about eight years old Gran and I pushed an old pram containing two milk churns to a nearby farm to ask for water. The farmer was very rude and shoved Gran who fell over and hurt her back as well as her pride. She was angry. Still on the ground, she looked up at the farmer and declared, 'By the end of the day you'll rue what you've done to me.' So saying, she delivered a curse in Romanes. Incensed, the farmer took a kick at her which I saw coming, so I kicked out at him. He hit me and knocked *me* to the ground. Gran and I got to our feet and walked about four or five miles to another farm. This time the farmer was kind and generous; he showed us to a standpipe and said, 'Help yourselves anytime you want water, there's no need to ask.' We thanked him and told him what had happened at the other farm, before heading home to the camp.

A few days later we needed more water so off we we
Having filled the churns, we were greeted by the friendly
farmer and Gran asked him how the other farmer was.

He told us, 'I'm glad you asked me that. I wanted to tell
you that on the day you were first here getting water he
overturned his tractor and broke both of his legs!'

A look of satisfaction came over Gran's face and she said,
'It ain't finished yet.' No more than that.

It was quite some time before we were back in the area.
The friendly farmer was still there and he had bought the
miserable farmer's farm for his son. He told us his neighbour
had had nothing but bad luck since the day he was cursed.
His crops didn't do very well, his horses always seemed to
go lame, the foxes killed most of his chickens and his cattle
caught an infection, so he had put his farm up for sale.
The only good thing that had happened, according to the
miserable farmer, was that his wife had left him: she'd run off
with a travelling salesman!

Gran was annoyed: a loud-mouthed, uncouth woman had
shouted at her in the vilest manner and had been spreading
stories about Gran being a witch and that she ought to be
hanged. One day Gran and I were sitting on the side of the
road near the camp when this woman came walking up
the lane towards the village. Gran stared at her but never
spoke and as the woman drew opposite us, looking more
than a little worried, she stopped. With a puzzled look on
her face, she tried to move forward but she couldn't. She
turned round, went back a few steps and tried again, but
she still couldn't get past us. She attempted it several more
times without success, eventually turning and heading for
the village by another way.

Gran stood up and beckoned me to follow her. Walking as quickly as her weight would allow, she took a shortcut across the muddy fields to reach the lane that the woman was now using to get to the shops. On turning the corner the now-frightened woman saw Gran again and again she couldn't walk past. She started to cry and pleaded with Gran to let her through. She asked if she said she was sorry, would that help? Gran never spoke to her, just kept her eyes on her.

The woman kept saying, 'Sorry, sorry, sorry, I won't call you names again, please let me past.'

Gran replied, 'I'm not stopping you, dearie, you're stopping yourself.'

Suddenly freed, the gossip scurried past us and headed to the village, no doubt to recount the happenings. Gran cackled with glee, showing her only tooth.

Gran eventually became the *Krallissi* (Gypsy Queen). Immediately after a woman had given birth they would go to Gran for her to tell the baby's life-fortune. Great importance was attached to her prediction, which nearly always came right. She would teach the young girls how to *dukker* (tell fortunes) by reading palms, by casting stones or small bones (Gran used the 'fox's head' from the base of a rabbit's spine), reading tea leaves, using cards or her favourite method, scrying – using the crystal ball.

Over the last few years there has been a religious revival among the Romany tribes right across the spectrum from Roman Catholicism to evangelicalism, and many Gypsies, including the well-known family of fortune-tellers the Petulengros, have given up making predictions as they say it is an insult to God. Others who tell fortunes disagree and say they have a gift *from* God and will use it.

Romanies are very good at reading body language and once they have gleaned some information from a *gorgio* whilst calling at their house to try to sell something or tell their fortune, this will be relayed to the next visiting Romany by putting a mark, which only another Gypsy will notice, on the nearest object to where the details were received. There are literally hundreds of marks, all with different meanings, that have been developed over the centuries. The next Romany to call will interpret the mark and will astound the householder with their knowledge and so some form of supernatural power is attributed to them.

I'm unable to make predictions in the way Gran did, although my eldest son and eldest daughter do. But something that happens to me, over which I have no control whatsoever (and I never know when it is going to happen) is that, whilst I am talking to someone, I will suddenly make a pronouncement, nothing to do with whatever we were talking about. We have a cousin named Kizaiah, who unfortunately had a terrible time with her husband. He tried to drown their eldest son in the bath, was sent to jail for many years and Kizzy divorced him. Because of the way she had been treated by her ex-husband, she had a breakdown, making it necessary for her to go into a mental hospital for treatment. When she came out she hated men and you had to be careful what you said to her; say the wrong thing and she would have a burst of outrage.

We – Kizzy, Maggy (my wife) and me – were sitting in the camp having a cup of coffee once when I suddenly looked at Kizzy and said, 'Kizzy, in twelve months' time you'll be married and having a baby.' I won't repeat what she said to that, but she is an earthy girl. She kicked the table over, upsetting the coffee cups, and stormed out of the camp. My wife said, 'Why on earth did you say that? You know what her attitude towards men is!' After a time the incident was forgotten until nearly a year later when Kizzy came to tell us she had met a man, fallen in love, was getting married and was having a baby. We were all pleased for her and I was especially pleased my prediction had come true. The downside to all this was that Kizzy went round all the neighbouring villages and all her relations telling them I was responsible for her baby!

2

THE CAMP

OUR CAMP WAS close to the Black Country. It was accessible
only by a single track leading from a small village, being
bordered on one side by a river and on the other by a canal.
The back of it was protected by a large marsh with deep
water and treacherous bogs. The area was known locally as
'Duck-hole', due to the large numbers of mallards breeding
in the marshes.

At the entrance two railway sleepers were used as posts on
which hung a pair of strong wrought-iron gates. These were
padlocked together every night. On either side of the gates
was a kennel housing a ferocious-looking dog whose barks
alerted all on the site. These guard dogs had been selectively
bred by crossing Great Dane types with boxer dog crosses,
eventually producing a large dog with a big head which
looked the part but was in fact fairly harmless.

The site consisted of several acres, part of which had been
drained and made a good hard-standing for many wagons
and trailers. There was also plenty of space for the horses to
graze. There was also an old bothy that had originally been
used by the navvies who had dug out the canal many years
before. The old building was situated right on the edge of
the camp at the end of a lane that led to the canal. Dad had

made a good job of converting several rooms in the bothy – a kitchen, living room and bedroom – so it was fit for habitation, and in fact my Mom often stayed by herself there. She didn't like to stay in a wagon or trailer.

Any travelling family was welcome on the site as long as they obeyed rules which were always explained to them on their arrival and strictly enforced by Dad. Although my Grandad lived on the site, he had handed all responsibility to Dad, effectively making Dad the *Sherengro* (Headman). Any major breach of the rules would result in the offending family being banished from the camp. Some of the conditions were: no cockfighting, dogfighting or any other blood sports; no fighting except for organised bouts; no undue mess (each family being responsible for the tidiness and cleanliness of their pitch); children to be courteous to their elders.

There had been Romanies on this pitch for many generations and they were accepted by the locals, who were not generally invited into the camp. Many local farmers benefited from having a pool of workers to do their seasonal work and from the Romanies' skills at breaking in and curing horses.

The camp was part transit and part permanent. Some families travelled extensively and used the site when passing through the area whilst others worked locally and only travelled short distances, returning every evening. There were families from many different Tribes, including some Irish Travellers. Mom came from County Cavan in Southern Ireland and Dad allowed her relatives to use the facilities when they needed somewhere to camp. They usually kept themselves to themselves and didn't really mix.

There were a large number of children and, children being what they are, a lot of mischief took place. The local bus service was run by the Midland Red and the route terminated near the camp. Quite often the driver and conductor went into the local cider house for a few pints before resuming their journey. This was too good an opportunity to miss. A rag or potato would be stuffed up the exhaust pipe of the bus and, no matter how hard the driver tried, the bus would not start. A telephone call would be made to the bus company's garage and an engineer in a truck would be dispatched from town, only to find (the rag having been removed), that the bus started without a problem, much to the bewilderment of the driver. After this had happened several times, the company caught on and either the driver or the conductor stayed with the bus whilst the other went to 'wet his whistle'.

One day, for some reason the gates to the camp had been left open and a large and imposing car drove into the camp. Two well-dressed men carrying clipboards got out. Children are very inquisitive and soon there was a throng surrounding the two strangers. The men asked to see the Headman. All the children were agog. Dad made his way over to them and as soon as the dreaded words 'School Inspectors' was heard – literally within ten to fifteen seconds – there wasn't a child to be seen. The gate was never left open again!

On another occasion, a little gang of us children were watching a field of huge pigs. Some of the sows were feeding their piglets, others were rootling about, some were snoring fast asleep, the boar was paying attention to the sows, as boars do. An old man and his extremely old dog came walking up the lane. The man kept waiting for his little dog as it was having great difficulty walking. We had a chat with the man while the old dog mooched about. Suddenly there was a loud yelp from the rheumaticky pooch and he went past us faster than a greyhound. He seemed to be heading back home as fast as he could go. The old man looked puzzled, took off his hat and scratched his head. 'Well I'll be buggered, I ain't sin 'im go like that for best part of some time.' We kids were killing ourselves laughing and the dog's owner joined in when we told him his dog had weed up the electric fence used to keep the pigs in. He had obviously had an electric shock transmitted up the water and into a tender part of his body. We found out later that no harm had been done but the dog would never go anywhere near a fence again.

When my cousin Kezz was sixteen and I was eleven, Kezz bought an ex-military Matchless motorbike. It hadn't got a pillion seat but this was overcome by welding a bracket onto the rear mudguard and tying a cushion on it. Rudimentary foot-rests were also added.

Kezz rarely spoke – he had inherited a family speech impediment which in his case manifested itself as a chronic stutter. At times it was upsetting to see and hear him trying to join in a conversation. Amazingly, he had a lovely singing voice without a trace of the stutter. Quite often he would 'sing' what he wanted to say. Being short, stocky and strong and quick to temper, it wasn't advisable to laugh at him, as many found out the hard way. Other members of the family had a very pronounced lisp or a slight slurring of the letter 's'. In my case, it was an inability to pronounce the letters 'r' 'l' and 'w' which made my speech sound babyish. Dad spent hours with me standing in front of him getting me to talk 'properly'. After two years or so, it paid dividends and I could speak normally. No one tried to help Kezz in the same way.

Kezz wanted me to come and see his motorbike; he beckoned me to sit on the pillion. It started first kick and off down the lane we went – no tax, no insurance, no driving licence. I'd never been on a motorbike before and I thought it was fantastic. Over the next few months we travelled all over the place; it was really exhilarating. He taught me to ride the bike as well and I rode it round and round the camp until Dad said, 'You're both making a bloody nuisance of yourselves with that damn bike. You are *not* to ride it in the camp again. Go up to one of the fields and use it there.' This we did and made an obstacle course and a lot of us had great fun. Occasionally, just for the devilment and excitement, I would ride the bike with Kezz on the back: out of the camp, down the lane, over the dog-leg canal bridge as far as the main road. One time I was about to turn round and head back up the lanes when a police patrol car went along the main road and the police officers noticed I was well under-age to be in charge of the motorbike. We realised they were braking and about to turn round and give chase. With Kezz urging me on, we sped along the lane, back over the canal bridge and careered along the towpath, left the bike in a spinney and walked carefully through the marsh to the camp. When we got back, Dad was talking to the two policemen from the patrol car. Having noticed us out of the corner of his eye and realising we must have left the bike somewhere off the camp, Dad said that there was no motorbike on the site and if they wished they could have a look round.

On the way out the policemen said, 'Whoever it is we'll get them, we're not stupid. We know it was two of your lads.' Then they drove off. We were cautious for a few days, then Kezz said, 'What speed do you reckon we can get over the canal bridge at?'

'Dunno, shall we try it?'

Kezz nodded his head so off we went. The bridge had a high hump and a dogleg to the right. We went over it cautiously at thirty miles an hour on our first go, then the second go we were at thirty-five when the handlebars scraped the wall and we wobbled to a stop. It was a clear run at forty, though Kezz had a job to control the bike after we'd got over the bridge.

'Shall we do it again, Kezz?' I asked him. He grinned and patted the pillion seat for me to get back on. We went as far as the main road to enable us to get a good run. Kezz throttled it up and off we went. I found out later we were doing nearly fifty miles an hour as we approached the bridge. There was an almighty bang as the bike hit the parapet and I remember sailing through the air towards some tall withy trees growing on the canalside and the next thing I recall was waking up in hospital with Dad looking down at me. I'd got a huge lump on the back of my head where I'd hit the tree trunk, three broken ribs and a broken arm. I asked how cousin Kezz was and Dad told me, 'He'll live but, by God, he's going to be sore.' Kezz had gone down the lane on his back and nearly scalped himself. From his neck up to the top of his head his skin and hair had been rolled up and the exposed flesh was full of gravel, as was his bum and his back. The back of his shirt and trousers had been shredded by the road surface and he had passed out because of the pain. The surgeons managed to sew his scalp back on, though he always had some bare patches where the hair never grew back. They also managed to remove all the gravel, some of which was deeply embedded, from his head, back and bottom. He had to lie on his stomach for several weeks.

Apparently a local farmer had been passing by and saw Kezz at the side of the road. He stopped to see how badly hurt Kezz was, then he heard a groaning noise from up in the trees and saw me stuck in the branches. The ambulance came and picked Kezz up. The problem was how to get me down from the tree. Several of my family came to help – a ladder was brought from the farm, Dad fetched a rope and small tarpaulin with eyelets and made a cradle and after a struggle they lowered me to the ground. I can't remember anything about it as each time I was moved I passed out with the pain. The motorbike had disappeared and wasn't found until many years later when the canal was dredged. We were lucky not to have finished up in the same place as the bike and been drowned.

After his operation Kezz was put in the bed next to me where he lay face down, swearing every time he moved. I was kept in for observation because of the large lump on the back of my head. At visiting time, much to the consternation of the ward sister, both our families came to visit us and took no notice of the 'Only two visitors to a bed' rule. They all took turns to visit us and there would be about ten of them round each of our beds. After a few days we both felt better and started to make each other laugh, so much so that we were warned about our behaviour. As we didn't take any notice, later that day two porters with trolleys, accompanied by the ward sister and several nurses, came into the ward and with very little ceremony Kezz and me were wheeled into a side ward for two. As she left the ward sister said with a twinkle in her eye, 'There you are, lads, you can laugh as much as you like in here. It couldn't have been very nice for you with all those old people. However, I expect they're as pleased as you to see you moving.'

I was discharged after a few days but Kezz stayed in the hospital for several weeks. From then on motorbikes were banned from the camp.

Although I was mischievous, I never did anything malicious to anyone, with one exception and that was the local gamekeeper. It had nothing to do with poaching. One day a small gang of us lads were on a little-used public footpath going through a wood with plenty of cover for his pheasants. As usual we were jackassing about when suddenly the gamekeeper came out of the bushes and accused us of trespassing in pursuit of game birds. We weren't and we strongly denied it, pointing out that we were on a public footpath. He called us insolent bastards and struck Seth, one of my small cousins, across the head. As if that wasn't bad enough, he then kicked Seth. He was a powerful man in his mid fifties with a liking for the booze. If he had done his job properly he wouldn't have lost so many pheasants. We could smell he'd been drinking.

I shouted, 'You're going to be sorry you've done that. My Uncle Reuben will knock nine colours of shit out of you, you bleeding big bully.'

He said, 'If you think I'm afeared of a few Gyppos, you're wrong. I'll take any of them on, anytime.' Then he walked off.

We picked up young Seth, who was still crying, calmed him down and decided that for the moment we wouldn't say anything. We would try and deal with it ourselves.

The next day me and four of my cousins got Uncle Reuben to buy us several strings of crow-scarers which, when the fuse was lit, would slowly smoulder and go off with a sound like a gunshot every fifteen to twenty minutes. At dusk, when we knew the gamekeeper would be in the pub, we planted the crow-scarers at the top of several tall ash trees which surrounded his isolated cottage. We waited for him to come back the worse for wear, watched till the lights went out, then scaled up the trees again, lit the fuses and hid in the ferns. The first loud bang went off after about twenty minutes, followed in quick succession by three more. The cottage lights came on and the keeper came running out, partly dressed. He stood listening, waiting for more shots so that he could work out where they were coming from. Around fifteen minutes later four more 'shots' duly rang out. The echo-effect made it difficult to determine where the bangs were coming from. We watched as he jumped into his van and drove to the gate, got out and tried to open it. He couldn't: we'd chained it in three places with some old locks and chains from Dad's workshop. We could hear him cursing. He drove back to the cottage and went inside, presumably to telephone the police, which he wouldn't be able to do because whilst he was at the pub we'd found the phone junction box and disconnected the wires. He ran back out in a terrible state – the bangs were going off, he couldn't get through the gate and he couldn't phone for help.

He shouted at the top of his voice, 'If you young bastards are listening, you won't get away with this. I'll see you in jail. You won't get away with it!'

We quickly went back to the camp and went to bed.

The police came the next day but it was a waste of their time – nobody knew anything. They were back again a few days later enquiring about another incident, but of course no one knew anything about that either. The second incident was this: we knew the gamekeeper's routine – he was a man of habit – and on a Thursday night he would leave the pub, drive for about a mile and turn down a steep farm track, stopping a little way from a spinney where most nights a large number of pheasants roosted. He would then sneak down and try and catch anyone poaching. This technique had resulted in quite a few prosecutions.

On this particular night we told Uncle Reuben what me and my cousins were planning to do and he agreed to help us. To make sure the gamekeeper stuck to his routine, just before pub-closing time Reub went into the cider house and said to Dad and a couple of his brothers, just loud enough for the gamekeeper (who was sitting by himself) to hear, 'I've just seen three of the village lads off up Sladd Lane. I bet they're making for the spinney.' On hearing this, the gamekeeper downed his pint and walked out.

Dad said, 'What's going on, Reub?'

'Young George will tell you all about it as soon as he gets back. I'm not saying anything here – walls have ears,' replied Reuben.

The gamekeeper, keen to catch the trespassers, reached the top of the farm track, switched off the lights and engine of the van, and freewheeled down the hill, picking up speed as he went. As he neared the spinney there was a terrific crash which caused him to lose control of the van. It veered off the track and ended up on its side in a ditch. Satisfied, the perpetrators moved quickly away from the scene.

The gamekeeper extricated himself from the battered van, shone his torch and realised he'd run into a big old rusty milk churn that had been filled with stones. The incident was reported to the police but they didn't get anywhere with their enquiries.

Unfortunately the gamekeeper's problems weren't over. Little Seth told his mom, my Aunty Asima, who told her husband, my Uncle Twelve Toes (real name Tobias Smith) who was also known as *Baulo* (Pig) because he had eight nipples in two rows of four down his chest and belly! He sought out the gamekeeper and beat him severely for what he'd done to his son.

It was only a few weeks later that a new, much younger gamekeeper appeared on the scene, the old one having taken another job in Lincolnshire. The new one, although young, was wise. He befriended the menfolk by visiting our camp and, through Dad, arranging a meeting. Most of the men attended; to start with they said nothing, only listened. The young man began by apologising for the behaviour of his predecessor – this went down well. Then he explained that he had a job to do and anyone caught poaching would be prosecuted, no first warning: all poachers would be prosecuted. There were mutterings and sullen looks from the men. Then he said that if the men agreed not to take any pheasants he would, after every fortnightly shoot, let us have the surplus which would vary from shoot to shoot including, if they were available, a few mallards. This was met with smiles of approval.

Dad said afterwards, 'He's a clever young man. First he lifted our spirits, then he put them down again, then finally he lifted them up again and finished off with something that pleased us all. Very clever – he's no fool – a man to respect and be wary of.'

The keeper was as good as his word: after every shoot pheasants were delivered to the camp. Some were badly shot up, but the bones could be used to make stock. The men kept their side of the agreement and a good relationship was formed.

3

DAD

DAD WAS A hard man physically, only five foot five inches tall but fourteen stone of sheer muscle. He was a former bare-fist champion, having had his last fight when he was sixty-seven – which he won! He was complex, a character of extremes, capable of being kind, loving and generous but also aggressive and vicious. He could be frightening when he was roused to anger. There was no shouting, ranting or raving; his response would be calculated, cold and devastating. To say he had a chip on his shoulder would be an understatement: it was more like a 500-year-old oak tree, due to the prejudice, harassment and bigotry that had been shown to him, a Gypsy of mixed blood, and his family wherever they travelled. He hated bullies and bigots and wouldn't tolerate any cruelty to animals.

In fact he hated cruelty of any sort. He always said there was never any need for it. He believed in killing animals for the pot but not for sport. No blood sports were allowed on the camp at all and anyone found indulging in them had to leave. Of course he couldn't prevent anyone doing anything they wanted once they were off the site and we all knew of farmers who allowed their isolated barns and outhouses to be used for such purposes. You could make a great deal of money if you were paid to allow hare coursing and lamping at night, although you risked jail, should you be caught. Several of my relatives had fighting birds, from bantams to big roosters, as well as fierce-looking dogs with bitten ears and many scars on their faces and bodies. The disgusting spectacle of cock and dogfighting is not for the faint-hearted. A lot of money changes hands but as usual it's the bookies that come out on top. In the bloodlust and excitement fights between the men regularly broke out as it's an extremely emotional time for them. I've seen a great big man from the Black Country howl his eyes out because his little bantam fighting cock had been killed.

Dad was a successful horse-breeder and dealer and was known and respected throughout the horse world for the quality of his 'coloured' horses, from ponies to heavy draught. Often he was called in by local farmers and stud farms to give his opinion on a sick or lame horse because of his knowledge of cures for animal ailments.

He always seemed to be working, with little time for leisure. Occasionally, though, he would take us to a fun fair. Once, when I was ten, we went with Dad, my best friend Sylvy (who had been 'promised' to me as my wife on the day we were both born) and two of Dad's brothers: Uncle George with two of his daughters, Angel and Scarlett, and Uncle Reuben. We loved the fair – the noise, lights, smells, rides, all the stalls and the glitz, just the buzz of excitement, candyfloss sticking to your nose, sticky toffee apples and crisp, sugary doughnuts. We had a go on the bumper cars, waltzers, high rides, water splash, rifle shooting and hoopla. Uncle Reuben won three teddy bears and gave one to each of the girls. Everyone was enjoying themselves. There was a good friendly atmosphere, despite the din of loud music, the people shouting and laughing, young girls screaming as they were thrown around on the rides.

The atmosphere soon changed when a group of five soldiers recognised us as Gypsies from our traditional clothes – wide-brimmed hats, collarless shirts, brightly coloured *diklos* (neckerchiefs) fastened with *sonneco fawnies* (gold rings), narrow-legged trousers and boots. They started to shout insults and obscenities at us. At first we tried to ignore it, but as the taunts got worse I could see Dad getting angry; George and Reuben were looking to him for a lead. A crowd quickly formed and watched to see what would happen. We were all about to leave when the squaddies went too far and the big corporal shouted, 'Cowards, are you? Hitler got it right – he should have exterminated all you thieving bastards.'

That was too much. Dad told Reuben to take us children back to the car and wait with the engine running. He told George that he would see to the big-mouthed corporal and that he, George, should go for the other big one. By now the crowd was quiet and there was a tingle of anticipation in the air. Dad and Uncle George were both wearing big heavy boots and as soon as they got close to the soldiers they both stomped as hard as they could on the soldiers' feet, causing a great deal of pain and probably breaking several toes. Both soldiers instinctively leaned forward towards the centre of the pain and as they did so Dad brought his knee up into the face of the big corporal, dislodging several teeth and leaving his jaw at a strange angle. George's head only moved about two inches before it collided with the other big soldier's nose, which shattered. The remaining soldiers turned and ran.

Dad and George left the fairground, got into the waiting car and we returned to our camp. As soon as we got back each man changed all their top clothes and hid the ones they had been wearing so that any description which might have been given to the police wouldn't fit. Uncle George pulled a big hat low down over his face to hide the lump and big bruise on his forehead and Dad was trying not to limp: Gran had removed one of the soldier's teeth from where it had been deeply embedded in Dad's knee, and it was painful to walk on.

The police arrived within an hour but all they found were a group of men sitting around a fire, singing and reminiscing about the 'old days'. According to each man, no one had left the camp. The police, realising it was a waste of their time as everyone had supported alibis, left, warning that they would probably be back. But they didn't follow it up.

When time allowed Dad would help one of Mom's cousins, Uncle Paddy, who had a contract with the river authority and canal company to pollard the willow trees along the banks of the West Midlands' waterways. Sylvy and I loved helping Dad and Uncle Paddy when they went pollarding. If the job was fairly close to the camp a decorated horse-drawn cart would be loaded up with all the necessary equipment – axes, hackers, double cross-cut saw, different types of sharpening stones and a couple of tarpaulins. If the contract was a fair distance we would use a Bedford TK Lorry. As part of the two men's wages for the work, they were permitted to keep some of the poles and they would use these to make posts, railings, gates and wattle-hurdles; from the smaller branches a variety of baskets would be made.

As soon as we arrived it was Sylvy's and my job to gather enough dry wood to start a fire. In fact there would be two fires, one to boil water and cook food on and the other to burn all the brash. Once we had the fires going and the *kekkavi wurmmelin* (kettle boiling), our next task was to erect a bender (tent) and make a shelter. We would select and cut to size quite a few suitable poles of willow. Then you'd push one end of a pole in the ground, bend it over and push the other end into the ground as well. Next you'd do the same with the other poles, all of them two feet apart from each other, until you had sufficient poles in a row to form the length of the bender. The height would be determined by the length of the pole and the distance between where the two ends went into the earth. The bent poles were then lashed to straight poles laid over them, using willow bark as the lash. This strengthened the structure. One tarpaulin was thrown over the top and another spread out inside.

We took food with us to cook but we loved to see if we could catch something – pheasant, rabbit, hare or maybe a duck or some other fowl to spit-roast over the fire. Generally rabbits were the easiest to catch. I'd normally use a catapult but if it was a nice warm day we would look for a likely place to find a rabbit basking in a tussock of grass or in the hedge. Then with care you could quickly put a hand inside and pull the rabbit out.

As well as lighting and maintaining the fires, making the bender and cooking the food, it was up to us to keep the site tidy by piling up all the wood chips and putting all the pollarded and trimmed branches into piles of different sizes.

All the tools were kept razor-sharp and were carefully honed. To show how sharp his axe or hackers were, Dad would wet the hairs on his arm and shave some off with one of his tools. Once when we were helping, towards the end of the day, the light was beginning to fade and Dad wanted to finish a tree. Probably feeling a bit tired, he swung his axe and on the downward swing it hit a *cag* (a small jutting-out branch) which deflected the axe and he dropped it. The blade sliced off both the side of his leather boot and his woollen sock, exposing the bare flesh of his foot which miraculously wasn't even cut. Another fraction of an inch and he would have been seriously maimed. Pale and shaking, he threw the axe to the ground, saying, 'Bugger finishing the tree, it can wait till tomorrow.'

Usually we took the wood chippings home to use on our fire as willow burns wet (although it spits). Halfway through one morning's work an elderly lady walked across the field from a row of tumbledown cottages nearby and asked if she could have some of the chippings for her fire. She was a poor old thing, shabbily dressed and in need of a good meal; she looked half-clammed. Uncle Paddy said to her, 'Come down late afternoon and you can have as many chippings as you want. I'll put some in hessian sacks for you.'

The old lady said her thanks and went back to her house. True to his word, Paddy filled several bags and left them in a stack. During the day, as we worked we moved further and further from the pile of chippings. About four o'clock we happened to look back and saw a man carrying one of the bags full of wood chips across the field. Dad and Uncle Paddy were up in the trees when I pointed out what was happening, and before Dad could say a word Paddy shouted, 'By the mother of Christ and all that's Holy, the bastard is stealing the old lady's wood.' He jumped down from the tree, screaming like a banshee and twirling his axe round and round his head, and he chased the thief across the field, crying, 'I'll take your head off your shoulders, you thieving bastard.' The man turned, saw this screaming madman gaining on him, and dropped the bag. He made towards the row of old cottages, running like a coursed hare, and disappeared up an entry. By the time the furious Irishman had run up the entry the thief was nowhere to be seen. Just as Paddy was about to give up the search, the old lady came out of one of the cottages and Paddy explained what had happened. With a gap-toothed grin she said, 'That was my son – I'd asked him to carry up the chippings for me.'

Shamefaced, Paddy apologised and asked if he could say sorry to her son.

'I don't think so. At the moment he's hiding under his bed and I don't think he'll come out until you've gone.'

Paddy carried a few more bags of wood chippings up to the house, for which the lady was very grateful and offered Paddy a crow pie she had made. Uncle Paddy gently refused. We all had a good laugh when Uncle Paddy told us what the story was. Then we tidied the site, loaded the poles onto the lorry, put out the fires and went back to the camp.

As a child I was very badly behaved – not wilful, just playing practical jokes which always got me into trouble, or running around as if I'd got a swarm of bees up my bum. Generally making a nuisance of myself. Dad would get exasperated, grab hold of me and say, 'If you don't behave yourself I'll send you to the Cottage Homes.' This was an orphanage for very poor children and alleged to be 'not a very nice place'. I didn't hear it as 'Cottage Homes', I thought he was saying 'Cotty Jones', so I referred to it as the 'Cotty' and soon everyone in the family called it the 'Cotty'. Dad, no doubt exaggerating, told me what it would be like if I was sent there, saying there wasn't much food and what there was wasn't very good.

Before and after school lessons everybody was expected to do cleaning tasks. And all the children had to get up at half past five and be in bed by eight o'clock. The regime was very strict and any misbehaviour was severely punished. He hoped that when I heard about the Cotty I would behave myself, not wanting to be sent there. I talked about it with Sylvy and we decided it must be the worst place in the world: but if ever I was sent there she said she would come with me. The threat of that place hung over me like a big cloud. Dad had only to look up and say, 'Cotty for you, my boy' and I would be quiet for a while until I forgot. But I was terrified of going to the orphanage.

One day when I was about seven or eight, I had driven poor Mom to distraction. She had suffered several major breakdowns in the past; now she was at the end of her tether and bordering on another. She went to my Dad and said, 'Get him out of my sight. I never want to see him again. I can't put up with him, he'll have to go.' With that she stormed off to the converted bothy.

Dad shook his head and said, 'What are we going to do with you, you young bugger?' Then he said, 'Your Uncle Shad and Aunty Lelinda are camping on the Gig.' (The Gig was an area of rough land where at one time there had been a gig mill which was used in the textile industry for napping woollen cloth.) 'Shall we walk over and see them? Sylvy can come as well. Go and ask her mom if it's ok.'

It was. Dad put a pack on his back and off we went. We had several miles to walk. The part I liked best was going through a great big wood. It was dark and mysterious and we played hide and seek and lots of other games. Halfway through we stopped, collected a lot of dry sticks and Dad lit a fire. We 'drummed up' (made a drink of tea), had something to eat and went on our way.

It was lovely to see our Uncle and Aunty and all their children again. There were three wagons, lots of coloured horses, bantam chickens and an assortment of dogs (mainly lurchers) and Dad noticed a couple of fighting dogs kept penned up separately. Dad kept his counsel and said nothing; he hated cruel sports and would not brook any such thing on his camp.

We were sitting around the fire talking when I felt hot breath on top of my head. I turned and there behind me was the biggest, loveliest dog I have ever seen. As I looked at him a great big tongue slobbered all over my face, covering it with drool. Uncle Shad shouted, '*Alay, Beng*' ('Down, Satan') and the huge dog lay down. Aunty Lelinda told us the dog was good for nothing, all he did was eat. It was a cross between a Great Dane and a Greyhound/Great Dane. Uncle agreed he was useless at *veshengreski chorin* (poaching), but he looked the part as a guard dog and he had been trained to growl and bark at the approach of strangers.

After socialising for a while it was suggested we have a walk around the Gig. Dad was chatting to Uncle Shad; Sylvy and me were running around with our cousins. We were drawing nearer to some formidable blocks of buildings. My cousins didn't know what they were, so I shouted to my Dad to ask him and he replied, 'The Cottage Homes'.

Suddenly I knew why we were going there – to leave me. It was obvious. Dad had a pack on his back with my belongings. Uncle Shad was going to help Dad get me into this hellhole. I told Sylvy and off we went in the opposite direction, with me shouting, 'You ain't gonna get me in the bleeding Cotty. I hate you. I ain't goin' in the Cotty.' Panic-stricken and with Sylvy following, I ran across the scrubland, away from the Cotty, heading back to the camp where Aunty Lelinda was.

Dad and Uncle Shad chased after us, crying, 'You're not going in the Cotty, I promise. Don't run away, you're not going in the Cotty.' I didn't believe him.

The two men were gaining on us as we ran across the rough ground, heading for a huge patch of brambles with a tree in the middle of it. Seeing an animal track going through the brambles (I later found out there was a badger sett near the tree), we dropped onto our hands and knees and crawled into the middle. Dad and Uncle Shad were too big to follow us. They walked round the edge of the briars, urging us to come out and both promising we were not being taken to the Cotty. Dad held up the contents of the pack so that I could see there was nothing belonging to me. I still didn't trust him and decided to stay put; I was safe there for the moment. No amount of coaxing would get us to move.

Unseen by us, Dad went to a row of nearby workers' cottages and explained to three men who were doing their garden what had happened and asked if they would help. They all agreed and brought long-handled brushing hooks. They lent Dad and Uncle Shad one each as well. The bramble patch grew smaller and smaller and the men got nearer and nearer, and eventually we had nowhere left to hide. We tried to run off again, but Dad caught me and one of the local men caught Sylvy. All this time Dad had been trying to persuade me I wasn't going to be sent away from home. I began to stop struggling and although I didn't want to do it in front of Sylvy I burst out crying in sheer relief. Sylvy started to cry as well. Back at the camp, we both sat close by my Dad in front of the fire whilst Aunty Lelinda prepared a meal and a hot drink for us.

Dad held me in front of him with Sylvy by my side and said, 'I'm sorry, I am really sorry you've been upset. I was never taking you to the Cotty. We were honestly just going for a walk and I promise you, you will never, *never* be sent to that place, ever. I give you my word. From now on we won't mention it again but I want you to promise me you'll try hard to behave yourself.' I promised to try. As we were about to start back to our camp I heard Uncle Shad say to Dad, 'What do you expect from him, he's a chip off the old block!'

One time when I was supposed to be helping Dad with some beet-singling, which is back breaking work, I took a rest. I picked up a small clot of soil and threw it at my Dad.

'That's enough. Go and get some wood and light a fire. We'll drum up,' he said.

'In a minute,' and I picked up another clot and threw it, hitting Dad's hoe.

'You'll be in trouble if you do that again,' he shouted, attracting the attention of the other hoers.

'You'll have to catch me first, old 'un,' I cheekily retorted. A few minutes later I chucked another clod and it hit Dad on top of the head. There was no reaction! I was all ready to run but he just carried on hoeing.

Ten to fifteen minutes later, Dad said he needed to pop over the hedge and would I keep an eye on his jacket? I said I would and watched him go through the gate into another field. Kicking the ground and daydreaming, I suddenly became aware that all the other hoers were standing up watching something. I turned towards where they were looking and saw Dad about ten yards away from me and bearing down fast. He had gone round the other side of the hedge, found a gap and was coming behind me. I turned to run as he tried to grab me. I tripped over his jacket and hoe and fell flat on my face. There was no time for Dad to stop and he fell over me; as he'd been running fast to get me he rolled over a couple of times and winded himself. Before he could recover, I was off across the field like a scalded cat, leaving all the hoers hooting with laughter. For the rest of the afternoon I kept out of his way. It was getting dark by the time he finished. He walked to his lorry carrying both our hoes, put them in the back, got in the cab and drove out of the field. I ran across the rows, expecting him to be waiting down the lane for me. He wasn't, he'd gone back to the camp, which was five miles away, and I had to walk home. When I got back there was no sign of him. He'd gone down to the cider house and the trailer where I lived with Dad was locked. It started to rain so I wrapped myself up in a tarpaulin and went to sleep under an old wagon. By the morning he had calmed down but as I approached him he looked at me, saying, 'One of these days I'll swing for you, you little bugger. Come on, let's go hoeing and no more buggering about.'

Most of Dad's relatives didn't like Mom – 'too many airs and graces,' they'd say. Mom was an Irish Traveller with Romany roots from County Cavan in southern Ireland. Dad had met her when he went over to the horse fair at Ballinasloe in County Galway. She was a lot younger than Dad but became his second wife, his first having died in childbirth along with her baby some years before. Mom's family had lived in houses for generations although they kept up their other Romany traditions. Even amongst her own relations there was a lot of jealousy as her family had a big house with plenty of land back in County Cavan. She had been given a good education at a private school. The one thing everyone agreed on was that she was a very good cook, especially her sweet baking.

Like most young lads, I was always hungry and when Mom was at home she would make lovely cakes, jam tarts and my favourite lemon curd tarts.

She had a few friends in the village who would call to see her for a cup of tea, a cake and a chat. One afternoon visitors were expected so a fresh batch of lemon curd tarts had been made. I asked if I could have one, only to be told, 'No you can't. They're for Mrs Cox and Mrs Blackmore.' I pleaded with her but she wouldn't relent. I sneaked into the kitchen when I thought her back was turned, only to be clouted on the back of the head with a ladle. Clutching my head, I vowed I'd have one of those tarts. Mom must have anticipated my thoughts and locked them in a small side room she used as a larder. Then she put the key into her *joddakaye* (pinny) pocket.

I was more than a little miffed at my failure to get a tart so I went round to have a look at the small larder window. I picked up an empty oil drum, positioned it under the window, climbed up and inspected the window more closely. It opened easily enough, but it was too small for me to get through. I could see the tarts but I couldn't get at them. Mom was in her living room so I took a fork, a brown paper bag and some string and put them in my pocket. Then I went around the camp looking for a pole about six or seven feet long. I found one on a pile Dad was going to use for making wattle hurdles. I tied the fork onto it, then, climbing on top of the oil drum, I eased the window open, pushed the pole with the fork attached through it, and skewered one of the tarts. Then I put it into the bag. Little did I know I was being watched by Dad and two of my Uncles – Dad had said, 'Keep quiet, let's see what the little sod is up to. He's always up to something.'

I had eight of the twenty-four tarts in the bag when I heard a noise behind me. I nearly fell off the drum: there was Dad, Uncle John and Isaac. I told Dad the story. He reached up and secured the window, took me off to one of his sheds and asked how many tarts I'd got. I told him eight so, looking at his brothers, he said, 'That's two each and not a word to anyone, all right?' I agreed. Later that afternoon Mom told Dad she thought there must be mice in the larder as eight tarts had been eaten. Dad said he would sort it out.

When Dad took the lurchers for a walk Sylvy and I usually went with him on condition we kept the noise to a minimum. We always seemed to see something interesting, like the time we were out rabbiting with the ferrets. We were waiting for the rabbit to be driven into the nets when Dad noticed two rats running down the track side by side. Before we could stop him, one of our terriers ran and killed one of the rats. Dad called the dog back and made him stay and sit. The other rat was squeaking and running round in circles and didn't run away as we approached. Dad pointed to the piece of twig the rat was carrying in his mouth: it was sticking out about six inches from the side of its mouth. That was when we realised that the surviving animal was blind and the one killed by the terrier had also been holding the stick and had been leading the blind one.

Another time we were going along the canal towpath when Dad held up his finger and went 'Psssst' quietly. That was a signal to freeze and keep quiet. Looking along the towpath, we saw a fox but we couldn't see what he was doing. Keeping perfectly still, the three of us watched intently, then Dad whispered, 'He's taking sheep's wool off the hedge.' By the time he'd finished, the fox was carrying quite a bit of wool in his mouth. Then he went to the canal bank where it had partly fallen away into the water and he slowly, oh so slowly, backed into the water. It must have taken him ten minutes or more before the water covered him nearly completely – only the tip of his nose was showing – then he let go of the bundle of wool, swam to the other side and ran off across the field. Dad got the wool out of the water and it was covered in fleas. The fox had been de-fleaing itself.

In the copse we've seen crows picking up wood ants with their beak, stretching out their wings and holding the ants against their feathers: the ants respond by squirting formic acid into the feathers, thus killing the crow's parasites. In another similar incident, a crow, who was among the many who came scavenging for titbits around the camp, was picking up the little pieces of bread we were throwing to it when Uncle Ezra tossed a still-smouldering cigarette end away. The crow dashed to it, picked it up, and much to our amazement spread out its wings and started to use the smoke to de-louse itself.

4

THE JUDGE'S FIELD

THE JOURNEY SO far had been uneventful except for the usual catcalls of 'Dirty Diddies' or 'Stinking Gyppos' as we passed through the villages and towns in our brightly coloured horse-drawn wagon.

We had travelled over a hundred miles in seven days. There was my Dad, my brother Jake and me, three piebald horses, two lurcher dogs and three terriers all making our way to visit Great Aunty Thurza who camped around the Peak District. It was mid-December and normally we would be at our winter camp but Dad had received word that old Thurza was dying and was asking for him.

The family had been travelling these routes for many generations and Dad knew every lane, stream, stopping place and probably every gateway. At the bottom of a steep hill we pulled onto the grass verge to give the horses a break before starting the long climb. It was past midday, the weather was closing in and the skies were heavy with snow. Jake quickly lit a fire and brewed tea that he sweetened with condensed milk. As we drank our tea it started to snow. For a few minutes small, fine flakes fell, then followed larger ones about the size of a half crown and it began to stick. It wasn't long before the surface of the road began to disappear under a covering of white.

The horses rested, we quickly linked the piebalds together so they could use all their strength to get the wagon up the hill. Dad held the lead horse and urged on the shaft horse while Jake was at the back, ready with the chocks to place under the wheels should the wagon start to move backwards. The pace was brisk until we were halfway up. Then, as we rounded a bend, the wind-driven snow hit us full in the face. The horses' hooves began to slip and slide but Dad, who had been handling horses all his life, spoke to them in a soft voice, coaxing them on to further effort.

About fifty yards from the top we saw a car nose-down in the deep gully by the side of the lane. Dad shouted at us not to stop – we would come back and investigate once we had reached the top. We crossed over the main road and followed a track until we came to an outcrop of rocks with a large overhang that provided shelter.

My brother Jake had been born deaf-mute but nature had tried to compensate by making him very strong with extraordinary powers of observation and a marksman's eye – he was a skilled shot with gun, bow, catapult and throwing knife. Using sign language, Dad instructed Jake to see to the horses and set up camp.

With hessian sacks over our shoulders to keep us dry, Dad and I made our way back to the crashed car. It was getting dark and the snow was starting to blizzard. Jumping down into the ditch, we peered into the car and could see someone trapped against the steering wheel, pinned by the rear seats which had become dislodged and fallen on top of the driver. After a lot of effort we wrenched the driver's door open and removed the seats to uncover a large elderly man whom we gently pulled from the wreckage. He was shivering from shock and pain, had a deep cut in his forehead and groaned every time he breathed. Dad looked inside the car and found a heavy overcoat and hat which he helped the man to put on and then we wrapped our sacks round his shoulders. He said he could walk but at every step he grimaced in discomfort. Slowly we made our way back to the camp. By the time we arrived back at the overhang all three of us were nigh on exhausted and frozen to the marrow.

The horses had been fed and groomed, a camp fire was alight and the stove in the wagon was drawing nicely with a singing kettle on top. The injured man sipped a cup of hot sweet tea whilst Dad cleaned and dressed the cut on his head. After removing his shirt and vest, we could see he was massively bruised all over his chest, ribs and belly. The medicine bag which we always carried with us was opened and a salve was gently rubbed into all the tender areas. From a small leather pouch a mixture of herbs was brewed into a tea, strained and offered to the injured man who drank it and then lay down on the bed in the warm wagon. We covered him with clean blankets and he soon dropped off to sleep: the sedative had worked well. During the night he periodically snored and puffed like an old grampus and didn't even wake up when we manhandled the wagon sideways on to the shelter to afford us further protection from the foul weather. Partly out of respect for the injured man and to give him some peace and quiet, but mainly because we wouldn't sleep in the same place as a *gorgio,* we put up a bender close to the fire for the three of us to sleep in and, after eating our meal of thick bacon slices and toasted bread, we settled down for the night.

The buffeting wind reached gale force, occasionally spooking the horses who were also sheltering under the overhanging rock. Despite keeping the fire alight all night it was very cold and the dawn was very welcome. At first light we could just about see through the driving snow that the whole landscape was covered by a thick blanket which had been whipped into deep drifts by the fierce wind. The storm was to last for a few more days.

Our new friend awoke in a confused state, the result of shock, pain and the sedating tea. He was very agitated and naturally concerned that his wife and family would be worrying about him. The situation was explained and we took him outside to see the conditions. He quickly realised it would be virtually impossible for any search party to be out looking for him. Dad promised that at the first opportunity we would try and get a message to his wife. He was a lovely man and seemed genuinely grateful for everything we were doing.

We found out from him that his name was John Harrison and he was a judge at the Assize Court. His house was five miles away across the other side of the valley. He was still in a great deal of discomfort, so, after he'd had a little to eat and drink, Dad gave him another drop of the herb tea, shortly after which Mr Harrison was soon sleeping again. 'While the mind rests, the body heals,' Dad said.

Eventually the storm abated. The wind had driven the snow against the hedges and into the lanes, forming impassable drifts but leaving most of the fields covered by only two to three feet of snow. Mr Harrison drew a sketch of where he lived and wrote a note to his wife. I was going to attempt to get to his house by way of the fields.

'Old Tom', a big heavy horse, dependable and placid, was harnessed and I set off, all the time looking for gateways or weak places in the stone walls. We encountered many drifts, some of which Tom pushed his way through. With others he waited patiently whilst I cleared a way through with a shovel. A few hours passed before we came out into a clear road at the edge of the small Peak District town. We made our way carefully through the narrow streets. The few people we did meet walked away when I tried to ask them for directions. The covering of snow made it difficult to follow Mr Harrison's map. Then I saw the church and knocked at the vicarage door. The vicar kindly telephoned Mrs Harrison to say I was on my way with good news. Slowly we climbed out of the other side of town to the judge's house, a large isolated place overlooking the valley.

I tethered Old Tom, gave him his bait bag and rang the doorbell. Two middle-aged men who were unmistakably Mr Harrison's sons opened the door. Although they had been forewarned by the vicar, they seemed rather alarmed at the sight of me. I was no doubt a peculiar spectacle, soaking wet, bedraggled, covered with sacking and blue with cold. I handed them the note from their father, by which time a kindly-looking elderly lady had come to the door. On reading the letter she burst into tears and threw her arms around me. The three of them plied me with questions but I was unable to answer due to my teeth chattering with the cold.

Standing in front of a roaring fire with my clothes steaming, I told them what had happened. The sons wanted to go and see their father straight away, but it was getting dark and starting to freeze and I refused to put Old Tom in any danger. Mrs Harrison agreed with me so it was arranged that we would go first thing in the morning, if the weather allowed. My horse was put into a spare stable, rubbed down, fed and watered and left to munch on a rack of fresh hay.

A hot bath had been run for me and some clothes belonging to Mr Harrison's grandson, who was just a bit bigger than me, were laid out. I wouldn't use the bath as it is considered *mochadi* (unclean) by Gypsies to sit in our own dirt, so I was shown how to operate the shower and this I enjoyed. Clean and dry, I ate a large meal after which, much to their consternation, I wouldn't use a bedroom, preferring to sleep in the stable with the horse.

When I woke the two sons had already saddled their horses and a few minutes later the three of us set back off to the wagon.

The reunion between father and sons was very emotional. Then a doctor came on horseback to inspect the injured man's wounds and he expressed great surprise at how well the cut on the judge's head had healed and at the power of the sedating tea. He told Mr Harrison and his sons that neither he nor any hospital could have done any better. This really pleased Dad.

The next morning there had been a sufficient thaw to enable a vehicle to fetch Mr Harrison, who left cosily wrapped and full of thanks and invitations to visit him and offers of help should we ever need it.

As soon as he had gone Dad unhitched his old bike from the back of the wagon and told us he was popping into town and would be back by midday. Jake and I were to clear up the site, harness the horses and make ready to move as soon as he got back. We did as instructed, then waited but Dad didn't return. By three o'clock we were getting worried – Dad had his faults but tardiness wasn't one of them. We unharnessed the horses and I signed to Jake to remain in the camp. I would ride Old Tom into town and look for Dad. I knew he had been going for provisions so I called at several grocers to see if they had seen him. Outside one of the stores I saw his bike and was told by the manager that he had been looking out of the window and saw two policemen arrest a Gypsy and take him off in a patrol car. I went to the police station and the officer on duty wouldn't tell me anything except to confirm that Dad had been arrested and was in the cells. I went back to the wagon and Jake and I spent a restless night worrying.

First thing in the morning I returned to the police station to see what I could find out. There was a sergeant on the desk and he told me that the Gypsy had been caught red-handed the previous night coming out of a house window and had been charged with house-breaking. I tried to tell the sergeant it couldn't have been Dad but he shouted at me, saying that all Gypsies are liars and thieves, slapped the side of my head and ordered me out.

Mr Harrison had offered help should we need it, so I went to his house and asked to see him. Mrs Harrison welcomed me in and fetched her husband who was accompanied by his youngest son. Both listened patiently to my story and asked me to leave it in their hands. Young Mr Harrison told me he was a solicitor and would go and see Dad and represent him in court.

When Dad appeared in front of the magistrates I sat in the public gallery and watched the proceedings. He looked pale and drawn; like most Gypsies he hated being confined in an enclosed space.

The two constables gave evidence against Dad, both referring to their pocketbooks, giving precise details of the time and date of the arrest and the circumstances leading up to it. The first witness on my Dad's behalf was the store manager who had seen my Dad being arrested by the two policemen at a different date and time to that stated. After being questioned closely by the magistrates, the witness stood down. The second person to give evidence for Dad was called – it was Mr Harrison the judge. He said that it was absolutely impossible for the two constables to have made the arrest when they said they did because the accused had been with him all that night and he explained how that had come about.

The magistrates didn't even retire, they found Dad 'Not Guilty' and he was free to go. On his release I hugged him tightly and cried. Although he always denied it, I noticed tears rolling down his cheeks too.

The two constables were ordered to surrender their pocketbooks and were suspended from duty immediately. Also confiscated were the custody records which had been kept by the sergeant. The subsequent enquiry found many errors, alterations and discrepancies in the notebooks and other records. All three were arrested and charged with conspiring to pervert the course of justice and remanded in custody until the next assizes where the former policemen were each sentenced to four and a half years imprisonment.

Through young Mr Harrison, Dad later sued the Chief Constable for wrongful arrest and false imprisonment and eventually received a handsome sum of money in an out of court settlement.

We eventually arrived at old Thurza's camping place two days before she died. She passed away contentedly after seeing my Dad and giving him, in true Gypsy fashion, a beautiful broad gold ring set with three diamonds which had belonged to her husband, Great Uncle Ezra. She had no male heirs and as Dad was now leader of the Tribe she had wanted him to have it, assuring him it was a 'lucky ring' and that as long as he wore it no harm would befall him.

The funeral was arranged and took place in a little stone church where old Thurza was laid to rest in the churchyard, overlooking the peaks she had always loved. At the funeral there were nearly two hundred Gypsy relatives and friends who had travelled from all over the country to show their respects to the Gypsy Queen. The men all wore black suits and trilbies and the women, their hair oiled and coiled, wore long black dresses and button-up boots and adorned themselves with old gold. After the funeral each man gave the vicar at least a five-pound note which both astonished and pleased him.

The ceremonial burning of Thurza's wagon took place and as the ceremony was ending a police car drew up and two big policemen walked across to the Gypsy gathering and asked for Dad. It turned out that Mr Harrison, who was well known to and very much respected by the police, had sought their help in locating us. He had asked them to deliver a message asking us to call and see him before we left the area. Being protective, all the Gypsy men silently encircled the policemen while the two of them talked to Dad. Dad looked round at them, smiled to show there wasn't a problem and waved them away. The message delivered, the policemen left.

We called at the judge's house the next morning and he asked us to follow him. Accompanied by his solicitor, he drove slowly up a narrow lane, turned down a track and stopped in a small field sheltered by woods and with a stream flowing through it. I watched from a respectful distance as the three men talked. I saw the solicitor take out several sheets of paper and Dad wrote on them. Afterwards they all shook hands. Mr Harrison came over and hugged me then drove off up the track. Dad was all smiles as he explained what had taken place. Because Dad had refused any reward, Mr

Harrison had instructed his solicitor to draw up documents transferring ownership of the small field to Dad. We could now use the site when we visited the Peaks without fear of being constantly moved on. Plenty of firewood, rabbits, game and water and sheltered from the wind by the trees. We were overjoyed and couldn't wait to get home and tell the rest of the family. Dad called the field *'Bistering manush poov'* (the Judge's Field).

5

GRANDAD

GRANDAD TOM, MY Dad's dad, was a small man, powerfully built, quiet and very good-natured. He tried to see the good in everyone. Even when the *gavvers* (police) came to raid us he'd say, 'Well, they've got a job to do' (and usually added, 'It's a pity they don't do it more fairly'). He said very little but listened a lot. Sometimes if you asked him a question you thought maybe he hadn't heard because he generally didn't answer at once. He had heard but he was considering his answer. He was, like many of us, a skilled poacher, never using cruelty and never taking out of season. His favourite meat was pheasant and I learned many different ways to catch them by going out with him. He would never use a gun: 'One shot and everybody including the *yogengro* (gamekeeper) and the *gavver* knows where you are.' Most of the time he would use a powerful catapult, an ash *forket* (furcate) with two strands of quarter-inch elastic attached to each side leading to a leather pouch. Wherever he went he would be on the lookout for pebbles of similar size and all weighing nearly the same; this was his ammunition for his catapult and what a good shot he was! I was in a spinney with him just after dusk one evening and silhouetted against the sky was a nide of roosting pheasants. Quietly he loaded his catapult with a stone, took aim, thud, one pheasant down, thud, another one, thud, number three. In all he took five and had been so quiet he didn't even disturb the rest of the sleeping birds.

He taught me that before you go out to *'chiv drey o pirri'* ('fill the pot' – in other words, poaching) you must know the lie of the land, and the strength of the gamekeeper and local policeman. Don't take risks else you'll finish up in the *stirapen* (jail).

Grandad would set snares for rabbits which he would generally check twice a day. I was with him once when he saw a hare in a field. It was too far away to get a good shot at it with the catapult but, much to my surprise, he did fire at the hare. He missed it by at least a couple of yards but it was enough to startle the hare which ran across the field and out through a hole in the hedge. We returned to the camp empty-handed, but I did notice Grandad go out again by himself a little later. Two days passed and as Grandad and I were passing the same field, there was the hare again. Grandad did exactly the same thing again and caused the hare to run to the gap in the hedge a second time. Quickly Grandad went across to where the hare had disappeared, picked up one freshly dead hare, slipped it into the large poacher's pocket in his jacket and made his way back to the camp. When he had gone out by himself, he had revisited the field, traced where the hare ran through the hedge and set a trap.

He showed me something else which I wouldn't have believed if I hadn't seen it with my own eyes. Spotting a hare lying low not too far away from where we were, he stuck his stick in the ground, hung his jacket on the stick, then slowly retreated. He told me to stay still and keep quiet. Next he skirted round the edge of the field, hidden by the hedge, until he was behind the animal. He walked across the field and grabbed the hare which let out a piercing scream like an injured child. It set my teeth on edge and quite upset me, but the captured hare was quickly dispatched. I marvelled at the way it had been caught and told Grandad I thought it was fantastic and did he think I could do it and how many times had he done it before? He said, 'So many questions,' then, looking at me, he said, 'I don't see why you couldn't do it. I'll let you into a secret: Cousin Manny told me that method, I've never tried it before.'

As well as our favourite plum brandy made with fruit from the trees around the camp, we also made a lot of wine, mainly from berries and grain. After fermentation and decanting, Grandad would put the wastings into a bag and set them aside. Then he'd take a stroll into 'pheasant country'. He would be looking to see where the birds went through a thicket into an open area in the middle of the bushes. When he had found such a place we would go back at dusk and he'd get me to wriggle under the bushes to the opening. I would have to pull the sack of wastings from the hooch behind me. Then it was my job to scatter the alcohol-soaked berries or grain all round the edge of the hidden grassy area. Soon the pheasants would find the 'treats' and start feasting on them. The more they ate the more intoxicated they became until some of them collapsed, absolutely stone-drunk. Later that day we would revisit the site, I would crawl through again and put the sozzled pheasants into a sack. Grandad would break their necks and then we would cautiously return to the camp.

There are many more ways of catching pheasants, most of which I have tried, but in the end I always went back to the trusty old 'catty'. Over the years I became just as skilful a shot as Grandad and my Dad. 'Should you wish to be a successful poacher, my boy,' Grandad would say, 'you need patience, skill and good powers of observation.' We would head to where we wished to bait a trap, set a snare or whatever it was we were going to use. Skirting around the field using the shadow of the hedge, we would make for the wood where we would stand still, listen and watch. Listen for the sound of someone pushing through the bushes or twigs snapping, watch to see if anything or anybody caused birds to rise into the air having been disturbed, or a bird such as the crow or pigeon flying overhead, seeing something or somebody on the ground and suddenly changing the direction of their flight. Once satisfied there was no one about, we could go about the business of taking game.

Once we were walking on a little-used public right of way, conveniently alongside a trout stream, when we bumped into the gamekeeper and bailiff with two spaniels. Unobserved, Grandad, who over the years had cultivated the habit of always carrying some cooked liver titbits (much loved by dogs) in his pocket, immediately dropped some onto the ground which were eaten by the dogs with much tail-wagging. The men challenged us and told us we were trespassing, an accusation which was withdrawn as soon as they realised we knew we were on a right of way. When they demanded to know who we were and where we came from, they were given well-rehearsed fictitious details, and having received a warning not to stray from the path we went on our way. The two men stood and watched us and we heard the gamekeeper say, 'I bet they're Gyppos. Some of them have pulled in to Fairy Glen. We'll have to watch those sods very carefully.' Then we went out of earshot (Fairy Glen was a large wood with dappled glades, and twisted and hollow trees where it was said fairies lived).

The light was beginning to fade when me and Grandad stealthily made our way back to the stream where he had noticed several places a trout might rest up and hide. We stood and waited under some trees for about twenty minutes or so, carefully listening. Then we set off along the path until Grandad suddenly stopped and moved quietly into the bushes. Holding his finger up (which meant keep perfectly still and listen), I could tell he was straining his ears, having heard something. We both concentrated and identified the sound more or less at the same time: two dogs panting. The gamekeeper's spaniels came right up to us in our hiding place and started to whine for some more titbits. Grandad gave them some – they were the same as they had had in the afternoon but mixed with them were a few different ones. The dogs quickly ate everything that was offered and Grandad gently pushed them away and very quietly told them, 'Go'. Being well-trained dogs, they left the bushes just as the gamekeeper went past. He called them to heel and they carried on away from us. Later Grandad explained to me that some of the titbits contained a harmless but quick-acting laxative which, once it started working, would keep the dogs fully occupied for the rest of the evening.

We had only gone a little way when we heard a loud splash and a cry from the keeper. I was about to run and help the man in the water, but Grandad held my arm and pulled me back. I found out later why we didn't go to the gamekeeper's rescue. 'It's an old trick,' Grandad said. 'I noticed a big log had been moved and placed nearer the water from where it was this afternoon and tonight the keeper picked it up and threw it into the stream. He cried out as if he had fallen in to see if anybody would go to his aid – then he's got you.' A lesson had been learnt.

Making sure no one was about, Grandad held a torch right on the surface of the water so none of the light escaped upwards but shone down into the water. After a short while a trout left the safety of its hiding place to investigate the underwater light. As soon as it did, Grandad quickly inserted his fingers into its gills and flipped it up onto the bank where he struck it on the head with a wooden mallet and popped it into a bag. We had two more fish and then made our way home.

As poachers we caught many things: *kavnengro* (hare), *shooshi* (rabbit), *barrikani* (pheasant), *bittikani* (partridge), *retchka* (duck), *wiffler* (pigeon), *barrimatho* (salmon), *orella* (trout) and *sappeskomatchi* (eels) – we love *sappeskomatchi goi* (eel pie). Eels live in streams, rivers, canals, lakes, ditches, drains and ponds – more or less anywhere there is water. They can be caught all year round but the best time is between May and September. An old saying is, 'When the willow comes into bud, the eels come out of the mud'. I've seen Grandad hold a wriggling eel, turn it onto its back, stroke its underside about two inches below its head and within a few seconds it had stopped wriggling and gone all floppy.

Grandad would set up lines along the canal bank to catch the eels, weighted so that the bait would lie on the bottom. These were checked daily and kept us with a regular supply of eels. In the wood at the back of the camp was a dank pool surrounded by bushes where we would sniggle for the eels by placing food in holes to attract the slippery fish, but Grandad's main way of catching them was a form of sniggling where he would make a bale of, say, bracken. In the middle he would place something that would attract his quarry, such as chicken innards or a rabbit paunch. Attached to a line and with heavy stones placed on each end, the bale would slowly sink and rest on the mud at the bottom of the pool. Drawn by the smell, the eels would wriggle their way into the bale and gorge themselves on the guts. Grandad would go back in the morning and lift out the bale which nearly always had several eels inside. He'd fashioned a small pit where he opened the bale: when the eels fell out the sheer sides would prevent them from escaping. Any small ones were returned to the pool.

On one occasion we were on our way to lift the bale when through the bushes we saw one of the villagers taking the eels from the bale and putting them in a creel. Grandad waited until the man had closed his basket, sneaked quietly through the bushes and pushed the startled man into the pool. Then he picked up the laden creel and we made our way back to the camp. The villager had no idea who had knocked him into the water or where his creel had gone but he had his suspicions.

When Gran and Grandad were quite old they were both poorly with bronchitis so the family temporarily rented an old cottage for them – they had a big fire burning in the grate but left all the doors and windows open. Grandad insisted on taking his horses with him and as there wasn't a gate into the large backyard the horses had to be taken through the house. Three of his animals were no trouble, but the fourth, recently acquired, was troublesome but eventually went through. After a couple of months they felt much better and decided to go back on the road which meant taking the horses back through the house again. As before, three of them went straight through without a hitch but the fourth, as yet unnamed, would not budge. Several members of the family tried to help but the horse dug his hooves in when he was pulled and lashed out if he was pushed; he wouldn't be coaxed, he was not going through the house.

Grandad disappeared for about half an hour then came back with a saucepan and told his helpers to get the horse as near to the door as possible and facing towards the way out. The awkward animal allowed himself to be taken right up to the doorway but still wouldn't go through. They were told to be ready to let go of the halter. Grandad went round the back of the horse which suddenly let out a loud grunt and galloped straight through the house and down the lane like a bolt of lightning. What Grandad had done was to boil a fairly big potato, then he went behind the horse, lifted up its tail and pushed the spud part-way up its backside. It had the desired effect. A few hours later they caught the animal none the worse for its experience and from then on it was known as Lightning!

In 1948 Grandad was seventy-nine, had no teeth and couldn't see very clearly, but for some reason he was very excited about this 'Natural Elf' he had heard talk of which was going to cure all their ills.

It was a Saturday morning. I called on Gran and Grandad and noticed a pony and trap had been made ready. Grandad was in his best clothes including 'a pound of lard' on his head to keep his hair in place.

'Where you off to, Grandad?' I asked.

To which he replied, 'I'm a'gooin into town to try and find that Natural Elf shop to get me some teeth so's I can 'ave summut decent to eat. Then I'm a'gooin in agen nex' wick to get me some glasses so's I can see what I'm a-bloody-eatin'.'

So saying, he trotted off to town. He returned a few hours later very disgruntled. 'No one's 'eard of the bloody place. I even went as far as asking a no-good *gavver.* He thought I was being funny and said if I didn't bugger off he'd arrest me for being drunk in charge. I knew that National Elf was a pack of lies as soon as I heard about it but I thought I would find out.'

Poor old Grandad died seven years later, still without any teeth or glasses.

6

THE CIDER HOUSE

A LITTLE WAY from our camp was the cider house right on the side of the canal, where members of my family used to drink. This place served no beer, no spirits, just cider – rough, medium or sweet – drawn straight from the barrel into crock mugs, topped up with a tot of illicitly brewed plum brandy ('*tatcho lyart purder!*' – 'a real mindblower!').

Any trouble was dealt with by the landlord, an ex-fighter from the Black Country, six foot four inches and twenty-six stone. Although most of his muscle had turned to fat over the years, he was still a force to be reckoned with, especially when he reached under the bar where he kept his shillelagh. He could clear the place in thirty seconds.

One evening we were playing Evesham quoits in the cider house when in came a local man, Bert Davies, who didn't like anybody and nobody liked him. Nothing was ever right; he complained constantly. His cup was most certainly always half-empty, never half-full. He walked with a very pronounced stoop which pushed his head out in front of his body and he was known as 'Ere's-me-'ed-me-arse-is-a-comin'. He loved playing quoits and was a very good player – he hated losing. The only time he hadn't got a fag sticking to his lower lip was when he was playing quoits. He would take his cigarette out of his mouth, dock it and put it behind his ear. He always wore a cap that was too big and he was continually pushing it back up off his ears.

One of my uncles threw down a challenge, so Bert went through his routine – cigarette out of mouth, dock it, put it behind his ear, adjust his hat. The game was well under way and for once Bert was losing, so he was concentrating even harder than usual. He was pitching a ring when one of my cousins nudged my Dad and pointed to Bert's hat from which a small plume of smoke was rising. He hadn't put his cigarette out properly, his hat had slipped over his ear and it was now on fire! Everybody noticed but no one said anything, they all dissolved into hysterics at the smoking hat. It put Bert off his game and he lost. He sat down muttering and had a swig of cider when small flames started to lick up the side of his hat. By now everybody was holding each other up. The flames got bigger so Dad poured a pint of cider over the burning hat. It all happened in a split second. Just as Dad poured the cider, another man lunged to grab Bert's hat off his head, but Bert had reacted to having the cider thrown over him and started to stand up. So because Bert had moved, instead of grabbing the hat the other man caught hold of his ear and yanked it, pulling Bert down to the floor. Purple with rage, Bert leapt to his feet and aimed a vicious kick at the man who'd knocked him to the floor, but he quickly jumped out of range so that Bert kicked a visiting drinker instead. This chap was carrying four pints of cider on a tray when he caught the kick right up the backside and he spilled the cider all over two boatman playing cards. They turned round to get their own back but the visitor had kept going so they ended up punching poor old Bert Davies between the eyes and knocking him to the floor again. They left in a hurry, vowing never to visit this 'mad house' ever again.

The place was in uproar and it took a long time for the laughter to subside and drinking to start again. Bert was helped up from the floor and partly pacified by being given a free pint of cider but he still left the cider house in a state of high dudgeon, pausing at the door to say, 'I only came in here for a quiet pint and a game of quoits and what did I get? I've had me ear nearly pulled off the side of me 'ed, I've ruined a nearly full fag, I've got two black eyes and I've burnt an 'ole in me 'at. And to make it wuss I lost at bloody quoits.' So saying, he walked out and slammed the door amidst gales of renewed laughter. Although this was nigh on fifty years ago it's still talked about to this day and is known as 'the smoking hat' or, to us, '*o tuving kaydi*'.

As well as being a place for drinking, the cider house was also a centre of entertainment. Behind the pub was a series of large outbuildings and a good-sized barn. One of the buildings had been converted into a ninepin skittle alley and another had a full-size snooker/billiards table, two dartboards and Evesham quoits. You could also play cards or dominoes and an area had been set aside for playing pitch and toss. Yet another had been converted into a gymnasium with a boxing ring where some of the local lads and my cousins and me used to train.

All these facilities and being right out in the country by the canal attracted people from the Black Country, many of whom worked in the steelworks and were hardened beer-drinkers. Charabancs used to come down on weekday evenings for special outings and 'do's', and at the weekends there would be several coachloads. Black Country pubs in the vicinity of the steelworks had extended licences so the men could slake their thirst and replace the fluid they'd lost through sweating as they worked at the furnaces. The men were used to drinking twenty pints of beer a day and when they first came down to our cider house they made the mistake of thinking the cider was weak. The landlord always asked if they were used to cider and advised caution. When he recommended they drank only two or three pints, this invariably caused much laughter. One new cider drinker declared, 'This stuff is like gnats' piss, it's like drinking water.' After he had drunk four or five pints a twelve-acre field wasn't big enough for him. His legs were like rubbery jelly; first he went forwards, then backwards, then sideways, finally falling on his head, saying, 'Me head's clear, I can think straight, but I can't control me legs.'

This sort of thing happened time after time. They soon got to respect the effect of a pint of cider. Generally there was little trouble and any that did start the landlord was quite capable of dealing with, but occasionally the mix of Gypsies, Black Country people, boatmen and locals turned volatile. An unfortunate remark chanced to be overheard, exception was taken to it and whoa! Up would go the tables and fists and feet would start flying. A few skulls would be rapped by the club-wielding pub owner and the troublemakers physically ejected. Usually it finished as abruptly as it started with a few men skulking away, nursing their wounds.

One such incident was sparked by a young man who had come down on a coach with his father. As he walked in he saw us and said to his Dad, 'Christ, the place is full of thieving Gyppos.' His father rounded on him and told him to keep his mouth shut. We had heard their remark, one which we had heard many times before. The majority of us ignored it but two of my cousins didn't and waited their chance. After the lad had drunk a couple of pints he was woozy and as he made his way to the outside toilets he was unsteady on his feet. My cousins, Ezra and Mordecai, casually walked out behind him, grabbed the unsuspecting lad and threw him in the canal, then calmly walked back in and started drinking as if nothing had happened.

Ten minutes passed, the door opened and in came a sodden, bedraggled young man, not smelling too good due to the smelly canal water. He was crying his eyes out and, on seeing my cousins, said to his Dad, 'They chucked me in the cut.' Everything went quiet. The landlord ordered the soaking wet boy outside. About twenty from the coach party stood up, fists clenched. Twenty Travellers stood up, ready to do battle. The landlord acted quickly and decisively. He placed himself between the two lots of men and brandished his shillelagh, saying, 'The first bugger that moves, I'll split his head open.' Pointing at Ezra and Mordi, he said, 'Out, both of you.' Then to the boy's father he said, 'Pick a mate, then the two of you go outside and sort it out. Nobody else gets involved. Drinks are on the house.' A big cheer went up and everybody rushed to the bar.

Once outside, Ezra challenged the boy's Dad and said, 'There's no need for Mordi and your mate to be involved.' The steelworker agreed, so Ezz and the Black Country man squared up. It was all over in seconds. The man grabbed hold of Mordi's waistcoat and yanked him forward. His head only moved a few inches before his forehead caught the top of Mordi's nose, spreading it over his face. Mordi went back to the camp where Gran set his nose; the other three returned to their drinking.

7

REUBEN

DAD WAS THE eldest and Reuben the youngest of Big Louie's eighteen children; twenty-eight years separated the two. Dad treated Reuben as a son and Reuben always looked to his older brother for help and guidance, especially when he was in trouble, which was often.

Reuben was a general dealer. He would deal in anything, straight or bent, as long as he could make a profit. Some of his deals were a little shady but he would never intentionally cheat or harm anyone. The local police knew of his activities but he'd never been caught. He had lots of contacts both within and outside the Traveller world and, should anyone have something to sell, chances are he would know someone who wanted to buy and for an introductory fee he would arrange the deal. As well as being a dealer he was a very good fighter, with or without the gloves, a skilful poacher, and had won many prizes at the Welsh trotting races.

Reuben didn't usually travel too much, only to the shows and fairs and on special occasions, preferring to conduct his business from the camp. He kept himself very fit and he had a well-honed body. With his long curly hair, big brown flashing eyes, lovely even white teeth and neat little moustache, he was attractive to the ladies, something he exploited to the full.

Always looking for opportunities to make money, when the local coalman let it be known he was giving up his business due to ill health, Reuben went to see him and, after weighing up all the 'for's and 'againsts', he bought the goodwill, constructed a storage compound on the site and fetched his supplies from a small mine in Shropshire. He did everything himself, fetching the coal, grading, bagging, loading and delivery. He delivered to quite a few villages and was generally well-received and popular. Despite some people who refused to use his services out of prejudice, he increased the customer base considerably. What was surprising was that he paid a bookkeeper and ran a legitimate business, presenting a set of books each year, probably to allay the suspicions of the taxman and hopefully prevent them from finding out about his 'other businesses'.

There was one customer on his coal round who he was pleased to lose. A snooty lady at one of the big houses had a fat, pampered Pekinese dog which used to bite Reuben's ankles. He told 'Mrs Snooty' about the biting and all she said was, 'My darling little Bertie wouldn't do such a thing, you horrible man. Just deliver the coal and go away.' This infuriated him, he hated being talked down to, but she was a good customer and always paid promptly. When the next delivery came round, it had been raining and the cobbles in Mrs Snooty's courtyard were slippery. Uncle Reuben was walking across the cobbles with a hundredweight of coal on his back when Bertie ran out of an outbuilding and bit his ankles. In trying to take evasive action Reuben slipped and dropped the bag of coal right on top of Bertie, who was killed instantly. Bertie's owner turned hysterical when she was told and she reported Reuben to the police. He explained to the police constable what had happened, and with much licking of an indelible pencil the constable laboriously made his notes and submitted the report to his HQ. It eventually came back marked, 'No crime or offence, no action necessary'. The policeman went to Mrs Snooty and told her that if she had kept the dog under control it would still have been alive to that day. The PC was duly reported to the Inspector, who ignored the complaint.

Although delivering coal is by its nature a dirty job, as a rule Reuben was very fastidious about his cleanliness and put clean clothes on every day. But one particular Friday, I noticed that at the start of his round there were only a few bags of coal on his lorry and he had on his dirtiest clothes from the day before. Also, he had deliberately rubbed coal dust onto his face, hands and arms so he was absolutely filthy from the outset. I didn't tell Reuben what I had noticed, but I told my Dad.

A month later Reuben did exactly the same thing again as this time both Dad and I watched unnoticed. Dad said, 'The young bugger's up to something. I don't know what the hell it could be – don't say anything to anybody else, I'll try and find out.'

Discreetly, Dad followed the coal lorry and after a few miles it turned into a long drive leading to a large and secluded home. The house belonged to a bigwig industrialist who had several factories in the Black Country. Watching from a distance, Dad saw his younger brother drop the coal down the cellar chute, then walk up to the front door, ring the bell and wait. After a few minutes the door was opened by a handsome middle-aged woman, with dyed blond hair and wearing a long white frock – Reuben then went in. Dad waited for an hour or so but Reuben didn't emerge, so he went back to the camp. Several hours later his brother turned up looking very pleased with himself. Dad didn't bring me into it, but he told Reuben what he had noticed about his appearance – he left out the part about following him. A guilty look crept over Reuben's face and he swore his eldest brother to secrecy, not knowing I was listening. Once a month, he told Dad, he delivered coal to The Firs – the house belonging to the pompous industrialist – after which Mrs Cox, the owner's wife, always dressed in pristine white, would let him in. Then they went down to the cellar where Mrs Cox would have laid out a white linen sheet, upon which, after she had removed all her clothes, she would lie down. Still in his filthy clothes and with dirty hands and face, Reuben would then make love to her for as long as she wanted. She would finish up as black as Reuben, then they'd have a bath. She paid Reuben several times the value of the coal and arranged to see again him the following month. Dad couldn't believe his ears and all he could say was, 'One of these days, as sure as eggs is eggs, you are going to get your fingers burnt and finish up in serious trouble.' Reuben just grinned and sauntered off whistling.

Reuben loved the ladies, the ladies loved Reuben. He never married, he had no need to! Should you happen to be in the village as the children were going to or coming from school, you couldn't fail to notice several children of mixed ages who looked like brothers and sisters. They were and they all looked very like Reuben, but they all had different mothers.

His coal-delivery business had expanded considerably but, not wanting to employ people to work for him, Reuben sold it on for a very good profit and put the money towards buying a magnificent Hereford bull which he leased to farmers to sire their cows. It was a beautiful beast and demand for its services was high. Reuben had moved from one successful enterprise to another and, as he said, 'By going to different parts of the country I meet a lot of farmers' wives and daughters.'

Gran and me were sitting on the steps of her wagon when we saw a village woman and her daughter crossing the camp. Mrs Oliver dragged her girl Winnie towards us and demanded to know where Reuben was. Gran replied that he was off travelling to a fair up north and wouldn't be back for a long time (he wasn't, he was lying down in the back of his lorry, hiding).

Mrs Oliver went on, 'Your Reuben has been with my Winnie and now she's in the family way. What are you going to do about it?'

Gran didn't answer straight away, she sat staring at the indignant woman who in her frustration snapped at Gran and again demanded to know the whereabouts of Reuben. To which Gran replied, 'I've already told you, he isn't here and, I repeat, I don't know when he'll be back, but let me remind you it takes two to make a baby.'

In high dudgeon Mrs Oliver turned on her heels, still dragging her daughter, and started to march back across the camp. They had only gone a few yards when Gran shouted, 'If it's any help to you, he charges twelve and sixpence for the bull.' Mrs Oliver was not amused and hurled a tirade of abuse at Louie, who cackled loudly.

Harry Slater was a big strong giant of a man but was not blessed with a quick mind. He was ponderous in thought and deed, generally accepting whatever he was told. His wife Vera was a lot younger than her husband, a well-made, attractive countrywoman with lovely 'come to bed' eyes. They had had four children in as many years and life was quite comfortable when in 1942, at the age of thirty-four, Harry was called up into the army. He was put in the Pioneer Corps to assist the Royal Engineers.

Reuben and Harry had become great drinking pals and as he left to go to the station Harry asked Reuben to look after Vera and make sure she was all right whilst he was away. So it wasn't long after Harry's departure that Reuben moved in, 'purely to look after Vera', he explained. Vera's husband became a prisoner of war and didn't return home for four years. When he did come home he was somewhat puzzled because when he had left he had had four children and now he had six.

The villagers waited in great anticipation to see what would happen but nothing did, at least not immediately. All was quiet for a couple of days, then Harry came to the camp and asked if he could have a private word with Dad.

'Tom,' he said, 'I need your help'.

'Okay,' said Dad, 'if I can help you, I will. What is it?'

'Well,' Harry started, 'when I went away I had four kids and now I've got six. I know I ain't the brightest person but I thought there must be something wrong, so I asked Vera how come she's had two more babies? And this is where I'm a bit flummoxed – she said she'd been visited twice by the Holy Spirit.' Dad kept a straight face as Harry continued. 'What do you think, Tom? Cos I don't know what to think, I don't want to upset my maker if it's true.'

'Harry,' said Dad, 'I'm not very good with things religious. What I suggest we do is go and ask Father Bartholomew and see what he says.'

'That's a good idea, Tom,' replied the cuckolded man.

So off they went together to see the vicar, who happened to be in the garden and saw the two men approaching. After passing the time of day and with the usual pleasantries, he listened intently and with hardly a change in his expression to what the puzzled Harry had got to say.

Father B, as he was known, didn't reply at once. He carefully packed his pipe, lit it, got it burning satisfactorily and had a few draws before he finally spoke. 'Harry, I've considered what you've told me and in my opinion I would be very surprised if God, who is the Holy Spirit, would visit your Vera twice. Once is a possibility because no one knows how Jesus will come to us again. Maybe it will be the same as last time and, with all due respect to you, Harry, in humble surroundings. But Harry, if you think about it carefully, there wouldn't be a need for the Holy Spirit to visit twice because once would be enough. I may be wrong of course. Now, before you go, let me say that your wife is a very attractive young lady, she's a good mother and up to the time you were called up she was a good wife to you. Let me ask you a question, Harry. When you were away from home were you ever lonely?'

'Ever such a lot, especially in the POW camp,' replied the now-thoughtful man.

'I expect you were,' agreed the vicar. 'But ... *but,*' emphasised Father Bartholomew, 'in the camp you had no temptation. So I want you to consider that Vera must have been as lonely as you, but temptation was there and someone took advantage of her loving nature. So think carefully about any action you decide to take because it could change your life completely. Do you understand what I'm saying?' Harry nodded. The vicar continued, 'So what I am saying is, I'm convinced it wasn't the Holy Spirit. I think you must look a little closer to home for the cause. And let me finish by adding that I think your wife is a lovely person, so please consider very, very carefully what you do.'

The three men stood in silence. No words were spoken for a while until Harry looked at Dad and the priest and said, 'She was lying to me, wasn't she?' Before any answer was given, he carried on, 'I know what happened, Tom. It's your bloody Reuben. He could talk the britches off a bleeding nun! When I asked him to look after Vera I didn't mean him to gid her a babby!'

Although the situation was serious for Harry, all three men burst out laughing at his turn of phrase, to which the churchman added, 'I quite agree with your assessment of Reuben, in fact I'd go one further and say he is quite capable of charming the knickers off the Mother Superior!'

On the way back to the village the wronged man said, 'Tom, I can't leave it there, I've got to have it out with him. Me and you've been friends for a long time but I don't want any interference from you or the rest of the family.'

Dad agreed but he also said, 'Keep yourself under control. Don't do anything you would regret because you might end up going away again, to jail.'

Harry wasn't really listening, he was trying to think how to handle the situation. As he entered the house, Vera gave him a sickly worried smile. Neither spoke. He took the six children to a neighbour's and asked her to look after them for a couple of hours as he needed to talk to his wife. Vera was trembling when he came back and she watched in trepidation as he carefully closed all the windows and locked the door.

Then he said to his wife, 'I don't like being made a laughing stock of. Those two babies had nothing to with the

Holy Spirit. You've made a bloody fool out of me. I trusted you and you've let me down, you've been lying abed with Reuben Locke. I understand you must have been lonely. I was as well. All I could think of was getting back home to you. A lot of other women were lonely but they didn't jump into bed with another man.'

So saying, he removed his leather belt, took hold of his quivering wife, pulled down her pants, put her across his knee and proceeded to smack her bare behind. After he had finished he ordered her to go upstairs and get into bed. Still crying, she meekly did as she was told. He followed her a short while afterwards and, as he later said to my Dad, 'I told her I still loved her, we would look after the two children as they needed a proper dad and it wouldn't be right to take them from their mum, but if ever she let me down again I would swing for her and she would be lying alongside her mother and father in the churchyard. Then I got into bed and showed her what it was like to have a real man again.'

Reuben had decided that discretion was the best part of valour and kept himself very much to himself. He could occasionally be seen skulking around the camp and Harry was keeping an eye out: eventually he spotted Reuben loading his belongings into his lorry. Within seconds Harry stood behind Reuben, tapped him on the shoulder and as he turned felled him with a mighty blow. Caught off guard, Reuben didn't stand a chance. The beating was long and painful and Reuben dropped to the floor looking a very sorry sight.

Having been ministered to and patched up by Louie, who offered not a shred of sympathy, with the help of his brothers Reuben loaded up his lorry, hitched up the trailer and without a word to anyone drove off to our relations in the Peak District. He wasn't seen again for two years.

All Gran said was, 'If the stupid bugger ain't learnt his lesson now he never will. I told him years ago if his brain worked as hard as other parts of his body he would be a millionaire.'

Harry and Vera's relationship eventually blossomed again, so much so that in the course of the next few years she had three more children – all of them Harry's!

8

COCKFIGHTING

WHEN I WAS nearly twelve (although I looked at least three years older), Uncle Reuben said *'Av aprey tawno yeck'* ('Come on young 'un') and beckoned for me to get into his pick-up truck.

'Where are we going?'

'You'll see,' was all he said. I wish he had told me because I wouldn't have gone. 'Your Dad knows you're with me but don't tell him where you've been when you get back, just say I was meeting a man about a few deals, okay?'

I agreed but I was always very wary of telling *hokkanos* (lies) to my Dad and hoped it wouldn't be necessary.

The back of the truck had been covered over with a timber structure with airholes drilled into the boards and a securely padlocked door. 'What's in the back, Reub?' I asked.

Reuben stroked the side of his nose, replying, 'For me to know and you to wonder. Don't worry, you'll find out.'

Alarm bells were beginning to sound but it was too late to get out as we'd already covered quite a few miles. We travelled about twenty-five miles into the Black Country and turned off down a rutted, badly surfaced track for about half a mile when we were stopped by several men who all looked as if they were from the same mould: thickset with shaven heads, cauliflower ears and flattened noses. I've seen prettier bulldogs when they're licking wee off nettles and even a warthog would have flinched at their lack of refinement. They peered inside the cab, demanded to know who we were and could we prove it? Uncle Reuben got out and soon had them laughing. He opened the door to the back of the truck and as the light flowed in two cocks began to crow. The men were satisfied – I wasn't. I told Reuben I didn't want to go and all he said was, 'It's too late now, our "friends" up there won't let you out until the show has finished, so relax and let's make some money. That's what it's all about.'

Dad hated cruel sports and wouldn't be very pleased to know I'd been to a cockfight. The contest had attracted men from all over the country, most of them with cages containing fighting cocks varying from bantam-size to nearly rooster-size. Other men had come to watch and place bets on the outcome. The venue was an old mine with plenty of hidden escape routes in the event of a raid. I wasn't looking forward to the spectacle of two cocks fighting but, apart from me, there was an air of excitement and anticipation.

As we were talking a large brightly coloured van with shiny chrome wheels and fittings drew alongside our truck and out got a man about the same age as Reuben. They greeted each other warmly and I was told it was my cousin Abner, Aunty Mizella's son. He was expensively dressed in a flash, colourful way; his clothes were obviously specially made. Two-tone Luton boots with high heels, tapered cord trousers with a traditional drop-down flap, crisp white collarless shirt with a bright red-and-white spotted *diklo* (neckerchief) secured by a three-diamond ring. His jacket was blue with three rows of white stitching round the edges and pockets, every button had been handmade out of bone. The whole outfit was topped off by a wide-brimmed, high-crowned hat. Reub told me afterwards that Abby was known as the *Barriporri* (Peacock) and he certainly strutted about like one. He had a lovely-looking silver, yellow and green fighting cock which also strutted around just like its owner.

Cocks are fought when they are aged one to two years. Each cock is heeled (its natural spurs cut down) and then artificial spurs anything from two to six inches long are attached to leather pads and strapped onto the cockerel's legs. 'Cutting out' usually takes place (trimming the wings at an angle, cutting down the tail and shortening the rump and hackle feathers, cutting the comb short against the head – all this diminishes the target offered to the opposing bird). The cocks cannot be touched once they have been placed in the pit, which is usually about eight feet in diameter and three to four feet deep to prevent the blood splashing onto the spectators. Should a bird refuse to fight it is set breast to breast with its opponent, and if it still refuses to fight it is regarded as the loser.

The artificial spurs that are strapped over the shortened natural spur are honed razor-sharp. Most fights only last a minute or two and quite often the winner also dies from its wounds. The owners take their birds into the ring and offer them up to each other and they are allowed to peck at each other's flaring neck feathers. Having their feathers pulled infuriates the birds, then they are put onto the floor of the pit and the fight begins.

The first main fight was due to take place shortly. Many pairs had already fought and the two main events were going to take place one after the other. The first of the big spectacles was to be a 'Battle Royal' which is when a number of birds specially selected for their stamina are set (placed in a pit) at the same time and stay there until only one, the winner, is left, the others having been killed or disabled. Cousin Abby's beautiful-looking cockerel came out the winner of the Battle Royal, which gave him a good amount of prize money, but that was nothing compared to how much he took off the bookmakers.

The last fight of the day was to be a 'Welsh main' where eight pairs were matched, then the eight winners were paired, then four and so on until the last surviving pair were matched. I had only seen one cockerel in Abby's van but at the beginning of the Welsh main he brought out another cockerel even more resplendent than the first. This one didn't need any encouragement to fight – he tried to peck anyone who came near to him. It was a really vicious bird who gave little chance to any of its four opponents. Again Abby won a considerable amount of money which he flaunted, much to the annoyance of many who had lost.

One of Uncle Reuben's cockerels had been successful and what with his prize money and returns on his bets he too had made quite a bit of money – only he kept his winnings quiet.

Although there was a lot of money to be made by rearing a good fighting bird or by betting wisely, the whole spectacle made me feel ill and I vowed never to watch another cockfight. Reub seemed pleased with the outcome but I told him I never wanted to go again. He apologised and agreed he should have given me the chance to say yes or no to going with him.

When we got back to the camp Dad was waiting and Uncle Reuben looked decidedly uncomfortable.

'Enjoyed the day?' Dad said to me.

Before I could answer Reub said, 'I've had a good day moneywise but the young 'un ain't enjoyed the day. Tom, don't ask him where he's been. I'll tell you about it later, ok?'

Dad nodded but I knew he had seen some feathers blow out the back of the pick-up.

At about five o'clock the next morning the camp was woken by the barking of the dogs chained near the gates, plus someone blowing a car hooter and the flashing of lights. Most of the men got up and the consensus was, 'It's the bloody *gavvers*,' but it wasn't. They all went down to the gates where they found Abby's van. Reuben went up to the vehicle, opened the door and Abby fell out. You could see by the half-light he had been severely beaten, he was a mess. By this time Gran had roused herself and demanded he be put into her wagon. Then we saw just how bad a state he was in. Not only had he had a severe beating and kicking, his clothes had all been ripped to slannocks, including his Luton boots which had been slashed.

Gran and Dad cleaned him up and dressed his wounds. He was made to drink some of Gran's knockout tea and he slept for twenty-four hours. When he came to, clean clothes were found for him and he tried to walk. He was very stiff and sore all over but at least he could now see out of both eyes. He told us that, after we had left the fight, he decided to follow us, but halfway up the lane he was stopped by six men jealous of his success who dragged him out of his van and started to thump and kick him, saying, 'You've taken our money, you arrogant bastard, now we're going to take it back.' He couldn't remember anything else until he recovered consciousness and all he could think of was to get to our camp. All his winnings had gone.

Abby insisted on going to inspect his van. All the windows had been smashed and there were many large dents in the bodywork. We opened the back doors, only to find someone had chopped the heads off Abby's cockerels.

He reached into the van, slid aside a wooden side panel and exposed a large amount of cash. '*Paracrow Devell lo kek komi latched dovo*' ('Thank God they never found that'), he said. 'I can buy me a set of new clothes and a new van and buy some more cocks, there's several thousand quid there.' Despite his painful ordeal, he was still showing off.

A few weeks later Reuben arranged for the family to look after his livestock, including the bull, saying he would be away for a couple of weeks. When asked where he was going, he did his irritating habit of tapping the side of his nose and grinning. All he would say was, 'I'm after some canary dogs.' Nothing more. I thought it was just another way for him to say, 'I'm not telling you,' and forgot about it.

Twelve days later he was back with four dog and four bitch puppies plus a three-year-old dog and a two-year-old bitch the likes of which I had never seen before. Reuben explained that they were called 'Presa Canarios' or 'Canary Dogs' so-called because they originated in the Canary Islands. The pups were gorgeous, it was quite unbelievable that they would grow up to be like the big dog, which Reuben had called '*Hammel*' (Attack). It had a massive head which was nearly as wide as it was long, with a large, powerful jaw and deep broad chest. The animal weighed about 130 pounds, had cropped ears and stood about two foot six inches to the shoulder.

Uncle Reuben said that they were fighting dogs. I found out that Reuben would travel more or less anywhere to get a good fighting dog. This time apparently Reuben had driven to South Wales, picked up a boat off the Pembrokeshire coast and, staying in close to the shore wherever possible, had made his way to Lisbon where he and his accomplices picked up the cargo of dogs and made their way back. Luckily for the dogs, they weren't challenged in the course of this journey, because I hate to think what would have happened to the animals if they had been. So they were brought into the country illegally, unquarantined and without a thought about rabies.

Reuben intended to breed and sell the pups. They proved very popular with the dogfighting fraternity. The demand for pups outstripped the supply and every pup was sold as soon as it was born – the dogs for fighting, the bitches for breeding. In partnership with the landlord of the cider house, he developed a thriving business. As Dad wouldn't allow any fighting dogs on the camp, they were kept in a compound at the back of the pub. They were well looked after, living in good conditions and well-fed and groomed.

Reub said to me, 'If ever you take one for a walk, always keep it on a lead with a strong reinforced collar and harness and never, ever let it walk in front of you. Keep it behind you or by the side of you at all times, then it will accept you as the pack leader. You must always dominate it or you could be in trouble.'

9

THE FIGHT

DAD DIDN'T EVEN look up or give any sign of acknowledgement as Jaunty Smith and his brother Awnie passed on their grandad's message asking for a meeting to discuss a fight between Jaunty and Reuben. They waited for an answer but as one wasn't forthcoming, they re-mounted their sulkies and moved off swiftly down the lane. The hatred between my Dad and old Bacca Smith was well-known and the thought of him made Dad spit contemptuously into the fire.

'The whole lot of them are the same, they think they should be crowing on top of the muck pile when they should be buried under it,' said Dad with venom.

Jaunty and his family shared a trait of arrogance, but even Dad grudgingly conceded that the young man was a very good fighter who would undoubtedly, one day, hold the area title – a title that Dad had held for twenty-three years, after taking it away from Bacca. That fight had been the most vicious, cruel and cold-blooded contest ever seen – no quarter asked, no quarter given.

Dad had been twenty-five, Bacca over forty. The fight had lasted twenty-five rounds before a new champion was proclaimed. When it was over Dad took months to recover.

Bacca had never got over it, he was mentally scarred – eaten up by hate – and physically scarred for the rest of his life, having been left with a permanently blind right eye and a grotesquely deformed nose.

Eventually Dad let old Bacca Smith know that he would meet him at eight o'clock in the cider house on a certain night.

Dad sat opposite the Smith family with my uncles. Nobody said a word, they all just quietly sipped their cider. After about twenty minutes Bacca said, 'I'm backing Jaunty to beat your Reuben and I'm willing to put up two hundred pounds. You lot put up the same amount, winner takes all.' No one spoke again for a full five minutes until Dad said, 'The purse isn't enough. If you think your boy can beat Reuben then make it worthwhile. Five hundred pounds, you cover it and I'll start making arrangements.'

Bacca was taken aback and his single beady eye flicked from one face to another. He'd thought two hundred pounds was a lot of money but he couldn't back down and lose face so he said 'Done'. Both men spat on their hands and slapped the other's. By this mixing of bodily fluid a binding contract was struck. In one month's time the purse of one thousand pounds was to be handed over to Big Jack the landlord for safekeeping. Any failure to do so, the fight would be called off and the family who reneged would be humiliated. Another meeting was set up, to take place after the money had been lodged with Big Jack.

Bacca and his relatives left immediately the deal had been struck. Dad ordered more cider, then turned to Reuben and asked him how long he would need to get into top shape.

Reuben answered, 'Three months.'

Dad shook his head. 'You need at least six months and that's what we'll stick out for, during which time, my boy, no booze, no fags and – *and*,' said Dad, emphasising the point, '*no* wenches'.

At thirty-eight Reuben was still in good fighting condition but fourteen years was a lot to give away. Jaunty was a good fighter, noted for his speed and devastating straight left. Reub was never short of money and was generous with it, especially to the girls, but should the fight go ahead his lifestyle would have to change as Dad and Uncle George would be training him and the regime would be strict.

Bacca was having trouble raising the stake. Ignoring the impact on his family, he sold a lot of their belongings: to fail to lodge the money with Jack the landlord would bring humiliation and scorn down on his head. In desperation he went to the October fair at Stow and put his most prized possession up for sale – a beautifully decorated and luxuriously fitted Reading wagon – but word had got around the community that he needed the cash so the offers for the *vardo* were very low. The highest offer he received was far below the true value of the wagon but to raise the money he reluctantly accepted.

The thousand pounds was duly placed in Big Jack's keeping and it was agreed the contest would take place in May – giving the fighters seven months to get into shape. It was also agreed that Dad would find a suitable venue and make the necessary arrangements. Bacca didn't want to know about the incidentals, he just wanted Jaunty to avenge the family honour. He didn't care whether the fight took place by the side of the canal or in the middle of a pig field, but Dad was canny and could see many ways of making money out of the event.

Excitement spread like a straw blaze around Gypsy encampments throughout the country and the prospect of a revenge fight between the two families was eagerly anticipated. So-called fight aficionados who had witnessed the contest when Bacca lost his title declared that this fight could be, if possible, even more vicious. Dad was aware of the great interest being shown and was determined to capitalise on it financially.

He rode out to see his old friend Colonel Todd-Pilling, who owned a large estate and a flourishing stable. This strange friendship between an ex-army officer and a Gypsy had formed when, out of desperation, the Colonel had asked Dad to look at a sick horse of his. The Colonel had explained that it was a favourite of his four grandchildren and that, after medical treatment had appeared to fail, the vets recommended it be put down.

Dad well remembered how the horse was lying down and showed little interest when he entered its box. He was listless and hadn't taken any food or water for some time. Dad inspected the horse and his droppings thoroughly and also looked at the type of food he had been eating and where it was stored. Finally, he walked round the paddock where the horse usually grazed. The Colonel asked if anything could be done for the animal. Dad said 'yes' and that he would come back in a few hours' time. He asked for the grandchildren to be there to help him administer the medicine.

When Dad returned there were four eager faces waiting for him, two boys aged fifteen and seven, and two girls aged thirteen and ten. They all went into the box and when he heard the children's voices the horse lifted his head. The Colonel watched while his grandchildren combed the horse's mane and gently groomed his back. Dad drenched the horse with some liquid medicine and then with the aid of a blow tube blew six medicinal balls down his throat. Next he spent a quarter of an hour gently rubbing and massaging the old horse's head and talking to him all the time in Romany. Eventually he stood up and said that the horse should be a lot better by the morning; he would pop back in early the next day to check on him. He also requested that the grandchildren, or at least the two eldest, stay with the horse, taking it in turns to talk to him. This, Dad stressed, was very important. The Colonel didn't query any of the instructions and made the necessary arrangements for them to be carried out.

At seven thirty the next morning a large shooting brake drew up at the camp. It was the Colonel and his two youngest grandchildren, who could hardly contain themselves. Politely they all waited to be asked to sit by the fire, then, before Dad could ask, the little boy shouted, 'Mr Gypsy Man, Cedric is on his feet and he's eating and drinking!' Then both the children ran to Dad and flung their arms round his legs and hugged him. They all went back to the stables together. When they went into the box Cedric put his head down and gently nudged Dad.

Dad said that in two days time Cedric should be led round the paddock with the young lad on his back. 'Just walk him,' he said, 'and then, in a few days, if he wants to trot let him but hold him back, don't let him canter. He's an old lad and he needs a lot of fuss, so put him in a double box and visit him and talk to him everyday.'

The Colonel offered Dad payment which he refused, saying, 'I'll chalk it up and if I ever need help I'll call and see you.'

The Colonel was very excited about the upcoming fight and, although he knew it was illegal and he stood a chance of being arrested, he nevertheless agreed to find a site somewhere on his large estate. He took Dad to look at an oxbow: it was ideal. This piece of land was within a 'U'-shaped bend of a river, so it had a narrow entrance, aiding crowd control, and opened into a large meadow. The river formed a natural barrier. The spot wasn't far from our camp and we quite often played in the wood nearby. This was where the fight would be held. It was also agreed that, after costs had been deducted, the entrance fee would be split sixty to forty in the Colonel's favour.

Reuben continued to train hard every day, under the watchful eye of his two elder brothers. By the time of the fight he was fully fit and raring to go.

Gypsies from all over the country had travelled to see the fight, pitching their trailers and *vardos* on any accessible spot. On the day of the contest people were making their way to the field three hours or more before the fight was due to begin. The cider tent was doing a roaring trade, as were the bookies.

The two fighters clambered through the ropes; the noise and hubbub from the crowd was at fever pitch. Jaunty, as arrogant as ever, danced, skipped and gave a demonstration of shadow-boxing. He looked in fine shape: broad shoulders, slim waist, muscles rippling, showing no sign of apprehension. Reuben, shorter and much thicker-set, also looked in good shape. Two of Jaunty's brothers were his corner men. Dad and Uncle George were in Reuben's corner, and they'd instructed him to keep on the move and not let his opponent settle into a rhythm.

The bell rang and Jaunty had hardly left his stool before Reuben sped across the ring and started raining blows to the head and body. Jaunty was completely taken aback at the quickness and ferocity of the attack; he could only cover up and hold on. A mighty blow caught Jaunty high up on the side of his head and dropped him to his knees. Up at eight, he back-pedalled as fast as he could. Surviving the first round, his corner worked on him, alarm and concern on their faces. In round two Jaunty expected Reuben to do the same and was ready; instead Reuben sauntered into the middle of the ring. This confused Jaunty — was it a ploy or had the older man taken too much out of himself? Jaunty decided he daren't take a chance and both fighters fought cautiously.

The third round was a repeat of the first with Reuben speeding across the ring and unsettling Jaunty, who defended himself well. At the start of the next Jaunty took the fight to his opponent, throwing caution to the wind. The two men traded blow for blow, slugging it out in the centre of the ring. Both received cuts to the face and head and blood splashed everywhere. The crowd loved it, they roared and shouted encouragement — this is what they had come for. They wanted blood, anybody's blood, as long as it wasn't their own.

The fifth was as ferocious as the previous round and an accidental clash of heads caused two split foreheads. Although both men were partially blinded by gushing blood, the pace was kept up, without any form of defence or skill — this was a pure trial of endurance.

During the break, Dad instructed his younger brother to fight cagily, not to slug it out. Jaunty must have been given similar advice and for the next few rounds both contestants fought with skill and canniness, but in the eleventh Reuben was suckered. Jaunty feinted with a right which the older man followed, only to walk into a devastating straight left which reduced his legs to rubber. For over a minute he hung on, frantically trying to clear his head. All Jaunty's supporters were baying for him to finish it. Three times Reuben dropped to one knee, taking a count of eight each time, depriving the younger man of victory. For the next round it was a case of Reuben staying out of trouble by using his ringcraft, chased by a frustrated Jaunty. The crowd booed and jeered, not liking what they saw.

Reuben had recovered by the start of the next round and came out full of passion. During a fine exchange, Jaunty accidentally delivered a very low blow which caused Reuben to drop to the floor, rolling in agony. Jaunty stepped back and apologised, expecting a stern warning from the referee, but to everybody's amazement the referee commenced to count to ten. The crowd erupted at the unfairness, especially those who had bet heavily on Reuben; at the end of the count there would be a riot. With quick thinking, the timekeeper rang the bell for the end of the round at least a minute early and didn't start the next round until two minutes had elapsed, giving the injured fighter time to regain some strength.

In the thirteenth Jaunty ripped into Reuben, cutting him to slannocks. Cuts opened above and below his eyes and he was bleeding profusely, but he wouldn't go down. One of the bookies was offering two to one on Jaunty winning and twenty to one on Reuben. There were not many takers for Reuben but Dad and Uncle George, much to the delight of the bookmaker, placed a hundred pounds on their brother. At the end of the round the battered fighter sank exhausted onto his stool, with little fight left in him. Dad performed an old Gypsy custom: he placed his forehead on his younger brother's forehead and they also touched fingertips, both with their eyes closed tightly. Dad spoke in Romany, saying the same thing over and over again, '*Lel tiro ruslipen fon mande*' ('Take your strength from me'): Dad was passing his strength to his brother. At the start of the fourteenth, which proved eventful, Dad looked pale and drawn but Reuben was revitalised.

At the bell Jaunty was looking for an opportunity to throw his straight left. Reuben, on instruction from Dad, was watching every move. Reuben played a dangerous game: halfway through the round, after Jaunty had delivered several good punches, he dropped his hands as if exhausted. Seeing this, Jaunty unleashed a mighty straight left with all his weight behind it. In a split second Reuben stooped and took the blow on the top of his head. The force of the punch sat him down but he had heard the sound of cracking bones: Jaunty had broken his hand on Reuben's thick skull. And now Reuben was up at six and stalking his opponent, who was now fighting one-handed.

The tension in the crowd was unbelievable. Between rounds I saw the bookmaker who Dad and Uncle George had used pass some money to one of the villagers; he then moved off towards the rear of the crowd.

At the bell Reuben fiercely attacked Jaunty, raining blows on him from all directions, and several times hitting Jaunty's broken hand, causing him massive pain. Following a bloody and sustained onslaught, Jaunty slowly sank onto his knees, pitched forward and fell onto his face, motionless. He was a beaten man.

In the noise that erupted a voice could be heard shouting 'Police' – it was the villager who'd been talking to the bookmaker. Pandemonium broke out and people ran in every direction, including the other bookies. I watched as the bookmaker we had used ran full tilt into a small spinney. When he came out he wasn't carrying his money bag. He staggered back into the fleeing crowd, shouting that he had been robbed. He was covered in mud and had a cut on his forehead. Unseen, I ran into the spinney myself and eventually found his satchel stuffed down a badger sett. Meanwhile most people had realised there wasn't actually a raid and had set off after the other bookies. Some sympathised with the one who had been robbed, others clamoured for their winnings. After I'd found the bag I'd noticed a disturbed patch of mud and blood on a tree trunk where the cheating bookmaker had inflicted his injury on himself. I ran to a hollow tree where I quite often played and hid the money in the trunk, then returned to my Dad saying nothing.

Jaunty was being tended to by his family and old Bacca was setting his grandson's broken hand. Reuben was badly cut and bruised, exhausted but cock-a-hoop.

The crooked bookmaker was giving details of the robbery and was describing his imaginary assailants.

That night Dad bought drinks all round in the cider house, where the main topic of conversation was the robbing of the bookmaker, with whom many people had placed large bets.

When Dad got home from the pub I told him what I'd done and we retrieved the bag and opened it in his workshop. There was a substantial amount of money. The first thing Dad did was pay his brother George and himself the money they were owed. Then, over the next few days, without saying where the money had come from, he paid out to everyone who had kept their betting slips; the residue he shared with his brothers, with some for me. The Colonel was more than satisfied with his share of the gate receipts.

10

UNCLE DEL (KNOCK)

FAMILIES WHO WORKED on the canal boats became known as water Gypsies because they were Travellers and a lot of their traditions were similar to the land Travellers. In reality very few Gypsies moved from the land to the water. One exception was my Dad's cousin Uncle Del (in the Gypsy community, all adult male relatives and close friends are given the courtesy title 'Uncle' and women are addressed as 'Aunty'). His real name was Enoch Smith, known as Knocker, then Knock and finally 'Del', which is a Romany word for 'knock' – so he became Uncle Del. He saw an opportunity, bought a narrowboat and plied his trade mainly round the Midlands, hauling all manner of cargoes including coal, vinegar, steel sheets, gravel, bricks and occasionally clays and ores for the pottery industry in Stoke-on-Trent.

Uncle Del was nigh on six foot tall and weighed a good twenty stone. His size made it difficult for him to be comfortable in the close confines of the cabin. On the surface he was jolly but underneath he could be devious and sly and he held grudges for a long, long time. Over the years he became well-known for breeding a 'boat dog' which was very popular with the boating community as they made excellent guard dogs. They were nicknamed 'Scruffies' and were a cross between a Staffordshire bull terrier and a Kerry Blue. Given the run of the boat, if they caught anyone pilfering they would inflict a nasty bite or bites and were worth their weight in gold for preventing losses due to thieving.

Del was helped by his wife, Aunty Beth, and whenever necessary one of his older children. The family lived in a tumbledown canalside cottage; they had numerous children and Uncle Del had been heard to say, 'You only have to throw your braces over the bed rail and she's having another baby.' No one seemed to know how many children they had but they seemed reasonably happy and well-fed, although their clothes were always unwashed and ragged. In contrast to Del, Aunty Beth was small – a dirty, smelly, emaciated old harridan. The first things you noticed about her were her extraordinarily big flappy ears and prominent Mr Punch nose and chin. If I had had a choice, I would much rather have been bitten by one of the Scruffies than by Beth as the risk of getting an infection would certainly have been higher from her.

As she travelled with her husband, the children were left to fend for themselves, the eldest being the substitute mom. At the earliest opportunity (from the age of six or seven), all the children were taught how to steer the boat – probably standing on a box to reach the tiller – keep it in a straight line, and get round a bend without running aground. They were expected to walk behind the horse to keep it going, and to learn how to lead it. The children were also taught how to groom, feed and care for the horse. Eventually, still at a young age, each child would be proficient enough to handle the boat, and they were expected to take over if one of their parents fell ill. While the boat was moving it was making money, when it was tied up it wasn't. Unfortunately, the children received little or no education, their world was the canal and the narrowboat.

Loading and unloading the cargoes was mainly done by the boatman himself and he was usually paid per ton of cargo delivered. From his wages he had to pay the crew – usually the wife and children, and as they were family they probably didn't get very much. They'd start work around four or five a.m., finishing some twelve to fifteen hours later. Depending on the distance of the journey, Uncle Del would occasionally work eighteen hours. A horse walking at a steady pace could cover about two and a half miles per hour so a journey time could be estimated in advance. The water Travellers being a somewhat 'closed' community, similar to the Gypsies, people became prejudiced against them. Uncle Del told us he thought when he changed from travelling the countryside to working on the canal there would be less 'predge-iss' but, as he said, 'That ain't so. If anything the predge-iss is greater.'

At times Sylvy and me were allowed to go on a trip with Del, sometimes staying on the boat overnight. Being so big, Del didn't sleep in the poky cabin but under canvas on the small deck or with the load. Before he cast off he would always point out the hazards and warn us to be careful. The water was the biggest hazard but you could be injured by the windlass flying off the paddle spindle or by getting your fingers trapped in the paddle gears. Ropes and lines could entangle limbs, fingers and feet and we were told to remember that horses can bite and kick.

We were going through a lock at Gailey on the Staffordshire and Worcestershire canal when Sylvy screamed, saying, 'There's someone in the water.' Uncle Del and me went quickly to have a look and there bobbing about in the water was a man's body. Uncle Del said, 'There's nothing we can do for him, he's dead,' and he told Sylvy to go into the cabin until we had gone through the lock. Uncle explained, 'We'll always stop and try to rescue a drowning person because it's proper and right and Christian to do so. But if it's a dead 'un, there's nothing we can do for them and if we stopped to get the body out we would have to report it and probably be called to give evidence at the inquest, which means the boat is tied up and I shouldn't be earning anything. That makes sense, don't it, my boy?' I agreed with him, although both Sylvy and I felt uncomfortable about leaving the body in the water.

On one occasion Beth and most of the children were very poorly. The only ones not ill were the twins, so Beth told Del he had to take the twins with him on the boat and get someone from the village to help him lead the horse and open the lock gates. Del was reluctant to be saddled with the two boys (who were aged about three), but Beth was adamant he should take them as she felt so ill. The only person he could get from the village was a young lad who was 'simple' but all he had to do was to walk with the horse and keep it going; Del would do the rest.

They started off at four-thirty in the morning, estimating that, with bait stops, it would be a sixteen-hour journey – plenty of time to get into the pub at the other end. Del was a hard-drinking man and he was well-supplied with homemade plum brandy with which to lace his cider. As was customary when young children were aboard, they were tied to the chimney so they wouldn't fall overboard. It was going to be an overnighter; the boat was due back late the following evening after picking up another load in the morning.

Darkness had fallen by the time they got back and the cottage was in darkness: Beth and the children still being poorly, they had all gone to bed. The simple lad made his way home to the village and Del spent that night in the cramped cabin. The next day was Sunday and there was no loading or unloading to do, so Uncle Del had a lie-in until he was woken by his wife asking where the twins were. At first Del was befuddled, still feeling the effects of the previous night's drinking, but his head soon cleared when Beth, although still feeling ill, flew at him, biting, kicking and screaming, 'Where are the twins?'

Uncle Del said he didn't know where they were, he'd forgotten all about them. Realising something terrible must have happened, Beth appeared to calm down and sent one of the children to ride to our camp and tell my Dad, as the *Sherengro*, to organise a search party. As soon as they heard the news, several uncles and cousins hurried to Beth and Del's cottage on horseback, with Dad taking command. On arrival they questioned the by-now distraught man as to when he had last seen the boys. He said that he remembered they were still tied to the chimney when he told the lad from the village to look after them and put them to bed and to stay with them in the cabin. Then Del had gone to the pub. Whether that was true we will never know. The lad from the village was gently questioned and coaxed to give answers, but all he did was grin and was no help at all. The men set off on their horses along the towpath, retracing the route taken by the boat two days before. They moved at a steady pace and scanned the water for any signs of the two boys. Every lock and sluice was looked into and lock-keepers questioned. Several miles from the cottage, Dad noticed that one of the keepers had light sandy hair and a slight cleft lip: the two boys they were looking for had light sandy hair and a slight cleft in the their upper lip. That's more than a coincidence, Dad thought.

The whole route had been retraced without success. The pub landlord remembered Del having a lot to drink and hardly being able to walk, apparently spending the night sleeping it off in a lean-to shed. Nothing was seen on the return journey. For several days men went up and down the canal looking for the boys and all canal-users were asked if they had seen anything of the twins but no one had. All the lock-keepers were asked to keep a lookout and also to question anybody on the canal. No official report was made, the closed community of the canal people kept it to themselves despite all the gossip and speculation as to what had happened to the two boys.

The relationship between Del and Beth floundered. She refused to work with him any more, so one of the eldest boys took her place and Uncle Del took to sleeping on the boat, cooking his own food and generally looking after himself. Once a week he moored alongside our camp and had his main meal of the week, always protesting his innocence and saying how he could never forgive himself. Quite often he began to cry.

Eight years had passed and I was doing a bit of scrap-dealing with Dad up in the Black Country when we found ourselves in the vicinity of the pub where the twins had gone missing. Making our way into the nearby town, Dad stopped the horse and pointed towards two young school boys aged about eleven. They were smartly dressed in what appeared to be grammar school blazers and each was carrying a satchel. Turning the cart round, we stopped a few yards in front of them, then Dad dismounted and approached the two lads.

He asked if they knew where a certain street was. They were very polite and well-mannered and directed Dad to the street. All the time Dad was looking at them intently and as he was doing so one of the boys took off his cap to scratch his head, exposing a mop of light sandy hair. They were identical twins and each had a slight cleft lip. Dad got back onto the cart and urged the horse forward, saying nothing for a few minutes. I knew what he was thinking. Turning to me, he said, 'Those were Beth's kids without a doubt. Do you know what I reckon?' Before I could answer he carried on, 'I reckon Del either sold them kids or he gave them away. He knew damn well they weren't his. I suppose another alternative is that someone heard them crying in the dark and took them. We'll never know for sure. Did you notice how smart and clean and tidy they were and how happy they seemed? It would be a tragedy for them if they were taken back to that hovel. I suggest we say nothing to anybody and I mean *anybody*.'

Although I agreed, I did tell Sylvy. I always shared everything with Sylvy. Dad and me were convinced Uncle Del knew where the boys were but it was too late for Beth, she'd died a couple of years since, raddled by booze. Coincidentally, only a few weeks after the sighting Del was found floating in the canal outside the cottage. A verdict of accidental death was recorded though many of us doubted that. Guilt is a terrible burden to bear.

11

COUSIN SCARLET'S WEDDING

WHEN I WAS eleven years old, Uncle George's daughter Scarlet was to marry Dalmon Smith. We all looked forward to a wedding – there would be relations and friends from all over the country, some of whom hadn't been seen for years. It was thought there could be as many as five hundred men, women and children at the celebration, all expecting a good feast. It had been decided they would have a quick church wedding and then return to the camp for a traditional Romany wedding. Gran wanted them to reintroduce the sort of wedding she'd had, but that hadn't been done for many a long year and, what's more, neither Scarlet nor Dalmon fancied weeing into a pewter pot. Neither did they fancy having their wrist or the palm of their hand cut so they could bind their marriage by the mixing of blood. They had two more choices: jumping over the broomstick or leaping over the brush. After talking about both ceremonies, Scarlet decided on jumping the broomstick. First of all she was told about the significance of the brush, but when she discovered that it's a phallic symbol (the stale, or handle, represents the male and the brush itself represents the female) and Dalmon laughed, Scarlet lived up to her name and turned bright red. It was explained to her with great delicacy – among Gypsies sex is never normally discussed in mixed company – but she dismissed that idea straight away. So jumping the broomstick was explained to her. Like many, Scarlet thought it was the same as jumping over the *brush*, but in fact it has nothing to do with broomsticks (in the sense of besoms, brooms or brushes). Instead it is a stick (branch) of the broom plant. Broom is supposed to enhance fertility. The yellow broom flower with its speck of red represents the blood spilt by a virgin on her wedding night, so the plant has become a symbol of fertility. A branch of broom bearing the sweet-scented flowers is placed on the floor (if the bloom is out of season a branch is cut from the bush and realistic wax flowers are added) and the couple 'leap the broomstick'. Should the bride's skirt touch the branch, this will show she has already lost her virginity or is pregnant and the man can then refuse to marry her. If the man's trousers should do the touching, this will indicate that he has been or will be unfaithful, and then it's up to the father of the bride to decide whether his daughter will continue with the marriage.

Everything was arranged for a Saturday at the end of October. Gran had predicted an Indian summer and said, 'The day will be full of sunshine and happiness.' Uncle George was hiring a large marquee which could have the sides rolled up so no one would feel claustrophobic. Barrels of cider would be trammelled on long tables with a plentiful supply of plum brandy. Cold meats consisting of venison, pheasant, rabbits and hares would be provided along with plenty of hot food – a mixed-meat *jogray* (stew) and a full pig roast. The butcher would be providing some of the meat, supplemented by what we caught ourselves by lamping for rabbits and hares and shooting a few roe deer. An order had been placed with the local bakers for a large quantity of breads and cakes.

As the day approached everyone was getting excited. Horse-drawn *vardos* and trailers of all shapes and sizes, pulled by vehicles of every make, started to arrive. Soon the whole camp was chock-a-block with visiting Romanies as was the field behind the cider house. Dad had greeted every new arrival and told them the camp rules, anyone breaking them would be sent packing and would not be allowed to attend the wedding. The landlord and his staff were run off their feet for the nights leading up to and immediately after the wedding. There were two other pubs in the village: one closed for the duration of the Romanies' stay and consequently lost a lot of money; the other welcomed the visitors and did a roaring trade, taking more in a week than they usually did in several months.

The *gavvers* were conspicuous by their absence: the local inspector had advised his constables to keep away and only go to the camp in an emergency and this policy worked well as there wasn't any antagonism. With so many people and so much booze, it was inevitable there would be a few fights, but these were quickly quelled by relations and peace resumed.

Three nights before the wedding was due to take place Dad, Uncle George, Jake, cousin John and me went lamping after rabbits and hares – I just went along for the ride. George, Uncle Jake and John stood in the back of the pick-up truck, Dad did the driving and I watched. A bar had been welded to the top of the cab onto which had been fastened several powerful adjustable lights. We had permission from the landowner as his land was overrun with rabbits and they caused a great deal of damage to his crops. Without any lights showing, we slowly cruised into the field until we heard a tap on the roof of the cab. Then Dad flicked the switch and all the cab-mounted lights came on and illuminated the rabbits. Each man had a .22 rifle and within just a few minutes we had bagged over twenty rabbits. The lights were doused until we had moved to another part of the field, then switched on again and more rabbits were taken and so on. At the end of the stint the catch was forty-eight rabbits, eleven hares and one roe deer – we weren't supposed to shoot the deer but, as George said, 'What the eye don't see the heart don't grieve over.' The rabbits were quickly paunched and skinned, the hares cleaned out (saving the blood for soup) and the roe deer jointed and wrapped in moist muslin.

After a further night of shooting we had enough meat to feed an army. Pheasants were purchased from the shooting syndicate and a large pig brought down from the village ready for slaughter. Dad and Uncle George killed the pig which was a noisy, messy affair; to make sure the poor old porker was dead some very hot water was poured down its ear – if the ear didn't flap it was dead. My job was to clean out the three miles (it seemed like that!) of intestines which were sold to the butcher to use as sausage skins and to make chitterlings.

Everything was in place: the booze was ready, the food was ready, the pig was roasting. Not long now before the celebrations.

The day of the marriage dawned bright and sunny and as the day progressed it became warmer and warmer. Gran was delighted and she lost no opportunity to tell everyone she met that she had predicted the beautiful weather over a month ago. The little village church was packed to capacity – every available space was taken and many more people stood outside to see the bride. Inside the church Dalmon waited nervously and the priest waited impatiently for the arrival of Scarlet. The volunteer organist, an elderly lady, played a medley of hymns. At times it sounded as if she had boxing gloves on, but nothing was going to be allowed to spoil the day. Most of the men wore sombre suits with collarless shirts and brightly coloured *diklos* and all stood on the same side of the nave. The women, resplendent in their showy, brightly coloured dresses, were on the other side of the aisle. In a huge white dress with a long train and heavy veil, Scarlet travelled from the camp to the church in a splendid landau drawn by four white horses. (Dad had won the carriage in a bet; when he got it the bodywork was very tatty but with quite a few hours of work he had brought it back to its original condition.) The top had been fully lowered and Uncle George sat looking very embarrassed whilst his daughter was loving every moment and waving to the passersby as she went.

The service went without a hitch. Dalmon had been taught how to sign his name – he couldn't read or write – and he was very proud when he signed the register. Back at the camp everything was prepared. The tables were groaning with food and the cider barrels tapped. The Romany marriage took place and the feasting and entertainment began. Everyone had their fill of food and drink and then settled down to watch competitions in dancing, singing, playing musical instruments (including fiddles made out of wire and cigar boxes), boxing, wrestling and the 'strongest man'. The music was provided by a Romany band called O Divi Jooks (the Mad Dogs) who played a mixture of traditional Gypsy, current popular ballads, country-and-western-style music and what would be described today as heavy metal mixed with rockabilly. Everyone had a fantastic time and it was agreed that it was the best wedding anyone had been to for many a year.

12

THE GENERAL

QUITE A FEW of the men from the camp did seasonal work
for the self-styled Lord of the Manor, Brigadier Henry
Montague-Somerville – known as 'the General' – who lived
in threadbare gentility in Montague Hall, which was about
a mile from our camp. It was a big rambling place in need of
urgent repair. He'd inherited the hall and about a thousand
acres of land when a cousin died. Apparently it was tradition
that the hall and lands were passed onto a male heir, so the
General inherited the estate – but not the money, which
went to the deceased relative's wife and daughters. The
General had some family wealth in the form of a trust fund
and also an army pension, having served in one of the Guards
regiments from the age of eighteen, resigning his commission
thirty-two years later with the rank of Brigadier. But he
employed a lot of farmworkers who lived in tied cottages
which he kept in good repair to the detriment of his own
property.

Rumours abounded about his private life (and of course
we Travellers are no different from the *gorgios* when it comes
to relishing a bit of tittle-tattle). Apparently, his first marriage
had come to an end when his wife left him for another man
because of his constant infidelity. Observing his behaviour

over the years did nothing to dispel the rumours. In the same year that his wife moved out, at the age of fifty-two he married a young lady thirty-four years younger than himself who, five months after their marriage, gave birth to their first daughter. She was followed over the next five years by two more girls and, eventually, a much-longed-for heir and son, christened Humphrey.

The General loved his horses and because of his lack of funds would always call Dad in to look at a sick horse: Dad was a damn sight cheaper than the vet. Any casual seasonal work that needed doing on the farm, such as beet- or mangold-singling, would be offered to Dad before anyone else and he would mark his scoot out where there weren't so many weeds (easier to hoe).

We would all help at *povengro-kettering* (potato-picking) and *boubi-kettering* (pea-picking). Potatoes were weighed in fifty-six pound bags whereas peas were weighed by the pot (an old unit equal to forty pounds). On many occasions people have taken a full bag of peas to the farmer for weighing and, before he's placed it on the scales, he's picked it up and said, 'Missus, there's a few stones in this bag. Take it back, empty the stones out and put more peas in. If you argue with me and I tip the pot out and find any stones, you'll be off the field.' Invariably the guilty party would take the bag back. Just by holding the bag of peas the farmer could tell if someone was cheating – he was used to judging the volume and he could spot if there were less peas than there should be.

One of his many idiosyncrasies was his tendency to refer to most men as 'barsterds'. 'Hello, you young *barsterd*,' he'd say, or he'd walk into the pub and say, 'Any of you barsterds want a drink?' In those days it was a grave insult to be called a bastard and it could easily cause a fight, but no one ever challenged the General, probably because he bought the drinks!

He had an eye for the ladies and most ladies liked the General. Tall, slim, kind, considerate and extremely charming, he had had many a casual affair with women in the village. 'Sixteen to sixty' was his motto and he lived by it.

Working for him on a casual basis was a woman named Lucy Pearce. Fat and unkempt, she always wore wellies no matter the weather, never any stockings, and she always looked grimy. Her husband was the estate carpenter and lived in one of the farm cottages, a very good craftsman when he was sober. Lucy liked the men and there were plenty of takers; the General liked Lucy, probably because she was an easy conquest.

When I was about ten, me and my cousin Caleb were fooling about just inside the wood not far from the camp when we noticed Mrs Pearce looking furtive as she made her way to an old wagon shed. Then we saw the General heading for the same place on his hunter. Caleb and me, keeping out of sight, ran to the old building, scaled the wall and looked down inside through a hole in the tiles. The General was giving Lucy a playful pat on the backside, then he said, 'Whenever you're ready, my dear.' Lucy Pearce undid the buttons of her dress and took it off. Then she lowered a pair of voluminous knickers down to her ankles – still not removing her wellies – and lay down on the straw. The General took off his multi-patched and darned tweed trousers, carefully folded them, laid them on the ground and stood there in his longjohns.

Caleb and me were scarlet-faced trying to suppress our laughter. 'Ready, my dear?' enquired the General, to which the casual farmworker nodded boredly. 'Good, good, then let battle commence!' Part-way through the 'battle', whilst the woman looked about her in an uninterested way, the General started muttering, 'Keep going, you barsterd, keep going, don't let me down.' Finally the battle was won and both put their discarded clothes back on. The General said, 'Thank you, my dear, very good, very good,' to which all she answered was, 'Ta'. As he was about to leave, he turned and told her, 'Don't worry, I'll see to the rent this month,' and with no expression of gratitude on her face she again just said, 'Ta', did the buttons up on her frock and wandered off back to work. Us two lads went back into the woods where we could hardly breathe for laughing as we imitated the General saying, 'Keep going, you barsterd, keep going.'

Brigadier Henry Montague-Somerville quite often visited our camp and would sit down and have a meal with us. Even Gran liked him and on one occasion she sent him an invitation to a special meal consisting of *zoomi* (soup) to start with, the main course being *i trim mas jogray* (a three-meat stew) followed by a *guyi* (pudding).

The evening of the meal came and everyone was on their best behaviour. Luckily it was a warm, dry, pleasant evening. The General in his dinner jacket and bow tie, accompanied by his wife in a flowing gown, drew up in their Daimler, alighted and took their places at a specially prepared table. Gran was using some of her best *scourdillas ta charos* (plates and dishes) and *churis, fongers ta rois* (knives, forks and spoons). You could see there were two sets, one slightly different from the other, and this was the set to be only used by *gorgios* and kept specially for such an occasion: we would never use crockery or cutlery used by a non-Gypsy as Romanies consider them to be *mochadi* (unclean). Everybody enjoyed the meal, our guests said how lovely and tasty everything was and thanked us for our hospitality.

The next day Brigadier Montague-Somerville called at the camp again as he was curious about what they had eaten, saying that whatever it was it had been absolutely delicious. When he was told he said, 'I don't think I'll tell Marianna. I'll say it was fish soup and rabbit, chicken and pheasant stew. She really did enjoy it but best she doesn't know it was snail soup, and hedgehog, squirrel and badger stew.'

The old General carried on philandering right up until the day he died at the age of seventy-eight and, true to form, his passing caused a scandal as he died in another woman's bed.

13

POLICE

DAD ALWAYS SAID, 'Once a copper always a copper. Never trust one and always watch them because they plant things.'

Nearly all Travellers have trouble with the *gavvers* at some time or another: it has always been so and will probably continue to be the case, despite a few senior officers trying to educate the rank-and-file police about travelling life. There is still far too much prejudice and bigotry shown by police and a sort of mutual hatred has grown up, accompanied by a willingness to flout the law and to take illegal actions on both sides, police and Romanies alike. During a raid on our Irish relatives' camp, one constable kicked over a big pot of *jogray* hanging on a tripod over the fire. It was very hot and some of it went over the children. Uncle Connor immediately knocked the offending policeman down and tipped the rest of the meat and gravy over him. Connor received six months 'down the line' (in prison). No action was taken against the police. With events like the above is it any wonder we dislike them as much as they dislike us?

Illegal raids on Traveller camps were a common occurrence and advantage was taken of the Gypsies' inability to read and their lack of knowledge about the law. One traffic officer pulled us over whilst we were travelling on a main road and said he had a warrant to search the wagon. When challenged, he produced a large piece of official-looking paper which was actually an invoice from a clothes store. I could read and so I told him he was a liar and that he'd be reported. Annoyed and also embarrassed, he sneered, 'My word against yours, Gyppo. Who do you think will be believed? We'll meet again.'

On another occasion two cars full of police arrived at the camp very early one morning when only a few men were up and rekindling their fires. An Inspector demanded to be let in, saying he had a warrant to search all the wagons and trailers. Dad being the *Sherengro*, he said to the officious policeman that there were upwards of thirty dwellings on the site and unless he had a separate search warrant for each one, named and detailed, he wasn't going to search any of them. Dad said he was welcome to search the grounds and open buildings by invitation, as long as every officer was accompanied to prevent any illegal action. The gates were undone and the police carried out a very ill-tempered search; nothing incriminating was found.

Grumpily the police returned to their vehicles, only to find all the tyres on both cars were flat. The Inspector became apoplectic with rage, threatening dire consequences, mass arrest and anything else he could think of. A group of the men had gathered by the gates and the mood was getting ugly. Dad challenged the officer in charge to state his proof as to who had let the tyres down – the Inspector couldn't. As Dad closed the gates he said, 'They've been cutting the hawthorn hedges, perhaps you've got a few punctures?' (Are policemen supposed to swear like that?)

Although it was well-known that some of Uncle Reuben's deals were a little on the shady side, he nevertheless developed a drinking relationship with the local bobby, Archie Grimes, who had been the village policeman for many years. Dad had warned Reuben to be careful but he didn't listen; every now and again he would say to Dad, 'See, nothing's happened yet,' to which Dad would reply, 'As sure as Hell's a mousetrap, it will.'

Once a week, when PC Grimes was officially off duty, he would drink in the cider house with Reuben. On other nights, as he did his rounds, he would pop in to a back room at the pub and have a few pints before going back on his beat. He was not particularly popular as he could be over-officious at times but then expect people to be friendly afterwards. He was also a cadger who expected and got free meat from the butchers, groceries from the village shop and free drinks at the pub. He always went on pub outings as well, and didn't expect to pay for either the coach or his cider on the trip – this annoyed a lot of the villagers but was no more than Dad expected from him. And as the landlord said, 'It's worth it as he tells me when the Sergeant or Inspector is visiting the area and I can be seen to be keeping lawful premises.' Most nights cider was still being served a couple of hours after closing time.

PC Grimes lived in a small police house with his wife, who was expected to look after the station in her husband's absence, and twelve children ranging from sixteen years old to a few months. Conditions were, to say the least, cramped and some of the children slept in a big shed in the garden and others slept in the two police cells (when there weren't any other occupants). A policeman's pay was very low but Mrs Grimes was a good housewife, not to mention the help of Reuben who made sure the Grimes had a good supply of rabbits and game in season. The children may have had clothes with darns on darns but their bellies were full.

One day one of my young cousins ran up, saying that PC Grimes was cycling up the track towards the camp. Within two or three minutes there wasn't a soul in sight. Sheds had been locked so he couldn't nose in and everyone had gone inside their wagons and trailers. Only my Dad and Reuben remained outside. Grimes nodded to Dad who returned the gesture but didn't speak. The policeman wanted a word with Reuben 'in private'. After the policeman had gone, Reuben told Dad he had given him a tip-off that the camp was going to be raided by the police early next morning and had advised him to shift anything dodgy. As it happened he hadn't got anything he needed to get rid of, but for reasons best known to himself he decided he didn't want to be on site when the raid took place (possibly something to do with a paternity order...).

At seven o'clock that evening Reuben announced that he was going to another Gypsy camp a few miles away and would stay there overnight. Instead of taking his motorbike, he decided to take his lorry as he thought he would 'kill two birds with one stone' – not too far from where he was going he had a load of scrap to pick up (a decision he was to regret). It was dropping down dark as he went down the track onto the lane leading to the village. Just by the top of the lane he was flagged down by two uniformed police officers who carefully examined his documents. Whilst this was going on some activity was also taking place at the rear of the lorry. The two police officers wouldn't let Reuben past to see what was happening. He soon found out. Two plain-clothed detectives came round from the rear of the lorry and asked why Reuben had a quantity of stolen copper piping on the back of his lorry. When he had left the camp his lorry had been completely empty. Reuben realised it was a set-up and that the two men with the copper pipes must have been concealed nearby, waiting for him. He denied everything but to no avail – he was arrested, cautioned, handcuffed and thrown into a police vehicle. The lorry was left on the side of the track. As he was being driven away, he glimpsed PC Grimes skulking in the trees. Reuben smiled sardonically, thinking, 'Tom was right – never trust a copper.'

Uncle Reuben was taken to the town police station, processed and locked in a cell. The next day, having no idea that anything untoward had befallen Reuben, all of us at the camp were up early in anticipation of the raid, which didn't happen. We were all talking about it when one of the locals drove into the camp in Reuben's lorry. He explained that he'd found it on the side of the track with the keys in the ignition – the bonnet was stone cold so it hadn't been driven for some time. Speculation was rife as to what had happened to Reuben. Many theories were mooted from his having been murdered over a bad deal to having been kidnapped by the jealous husband or boyfriend of one of his conquests.

The villager took us to where he had found the lorry and you could clearly see where two vehicles had been parked behind a hedge.

Uncle Isaac said, 'It's a good place for an ambush; you wouldn't see the parked cars when you were driving up the lane. It's probably the *gavvers*. Don't you think it's strange Grimes gave Reuben the tip-off about the raid? The *gavvers* were waiting, hoping Reuben would have some hot stuff to move. As it happened his lorry was empty but that wouldn't stop them fitting him up. Don't you think it's funny there wasn't a raid?'

Dad replied, 'If what you said's right, it was obviously a set-up. They've tried raiding the camp several times and never found anything to incriminate him. Now the bastards have got him by fixing him up. Let's go and see if we can find him.'

Everybody agreed; several Uncles went to the police station in Dad's lorry only to be told curtly by the desk sergeant that Reuben had been arrested for handling stolen goods and was appearing before the magistrates later that day. His case was referred to the assizes and Uncle Reuben was remanded in custody. At the assizes he was found guilty and sentenced to eighteen months in jail, of which he served twelve months. He spoke little of his experience. The first thing he did when he came out of prison was to visit one of his many girlfriends, even before he came back to the camp. As he said to Dad, 'A man needs his comforts!'

We all went down the pub to celebrate his release. When we arrived PC Grimes was in the bar and looked very uncomfortable and embarrassed. You could hear a pin drop and all eyes were on Reuben to see what he would do. Much to everyone's surprise he bought everyone a drink, including Grimes. Later the policeman took Reuben aside and told him he was sorry but that he had been under pressure from the detectives who'd threatened to inform on him about his drinking problem. Reuben listened but said nothing. Everything appeared to return to normal.

The next evening in the cider house the policeman was in the back room having his customary free pint when Reuben sent one through to him heavily laced with plum brandy. 'By God, that's a drop of good,' the local bobby declared, so Reuben sent another one through to the back room. By this time the on-duty policeman was getting very slurred and only weakly protested when two more pints of laced cider were taken to him. After drinking these he staggered outside and as soon as the fresh air hit him he went down like a 'toad from roost', as we used to say.

Uncle Reuben and a couple of his brothers carried the inebriated policeman to a bench by the side of the canal, laid him on it, folded his arms and placed a bunch of wild flowers in his hands. The police HQ received an anonymous telephone call saying that one of their officers appeared to be in a bad way and giving directions to where he could be found. It was gone ten o'clock when three police cars pulled up by the side of the canal and found the drunken policeman who was taken to hospital where they used a stomach pump on him. No one except PC Grimes knows what was said but within two days a new, young and very ambitious police officer had been installed. Later we found out that Grimes had been instantly dismissed and was now a bin man. He was living in a council house on an estate in town.

14

SYLVY

SYLVY AND I were born on the same day in wagons opposite each other (Mom's last two children were born only eleven months apart and apparently if a woman has two children within twelve months they are jokingly called 'Irish Twins'. Me being the youngest of the twins!). Within hours of my birth my Mom had another breakdown and was quickly whisked away to the local mental hospital where she remained for a long time.

Dad didn't know what to do, but Gran picked me up and took me into Milletti's wagon, where she was feeding Sylvy, and thrust me into her arms, saying, 'You've got two, put him on the other!' Dutifully, Milletti, who was Gran's niece and the only woman on the camp with milk, did as she was told – so Sylvy and me were suckled on the same breasts and put to lie in the same box. That was the beginning of an unbreakable bond between us. We went everywhere together, usually holding hands, travelling with each other's families so we wouldn't be separated. The first few years were idyllic but at the age of six I was told that from now on I would be spending most of the day with my Dad or one of my uncles to learn the skills of life that a Romany needs to exist. This was to make sure that when I became a man at sixteen I could get married and would be able to support a wife and children. Sylvy was to spend time with her mom or aunties in order to pick up all the duties expected of a woman, including selling door to door and learning the various ways of telling fortunes, in preparation for the day she would become a wife.

As soon as the work day had ended and we'd both finished our tasks we would be together again, either walking across the fields or sitting by the fire listening to stories about the old days, or to some of the men playing their homemade fiddles, penny whistles and accordions. Quite often someone would start singing or dancing.

Mom had had several severe breakdowns but none so bad as the one when I was in my twelfth year. I walked into her living room in the old bothy one day and saw her cavorting round and round the table, wild-eyed, hair dishevelled, arms flailing up and down, singing, laughing and crying all at the same time, tears dripping off the end of her chin. Unseeing, uncaring and unhearing, she was lost in a world of her own.

Suddenly she lunged past me and flung herself down onto an old couch, sobbing uncontrollably, her frock all rumpled up around her waist. After a short while I cautiously reached out and tried to adjust her dress, trying to preserve a little bit of her dignity.

I picked up everything I thought Mom might hurt herself with and locked it all in a shed. I told her I was going to fetch Dad but she gave no indication she had heard me. By now she was muttering incoherently with her face buried deep into the cushions. I quietly left and locked the door and hurried to the field where Dad was tending his horses.

He saw me coming, stood up from inspecting a horse's hoof and listened whilst I told him about Mom. He sadly shook his head and said, not unsympathetically, 'Oh Christ, not again.' We hurried back and on unlocking the door we found Mom sitting on a stool in the little kitchen, rocking backwards and forwards. Dad was a hard man but he couldn't disguise the pain in his eyes as he looked tenderly and pityingly at his wife. Within three hours she had been taken to the mental hospital again.

Dad had been planning quite a long trip away, including going across to Ireland to complete some horse deals. I was the sort of child everybody was pleased wasn't theirs – the last time Dad had been away, me and several cousins had just about avoided getting arrested. This time he was taking no chances, so he arranged with Sylvy's mom and dad for her to go with me to stay with an old aunt and uncle down in Wales. He said he didn't know how long we would be away for.

I'd stayed with them before and they were lovely people. Sylvy and I were both excited about going and were looking forward to the journey – we'd be travelling by ourselves. The day after Dad left, my Uncle Reuben took the two of us to the nearby railway station on the edge of the Black Country. Although it was nearly four years since the War had ended and the place was clean and tidy, the garden well-tended, even so the buildings needed painting and there was an air of dereliction. We paid for our third-class tickets and waited expectantly for the train that would take us to the Welsh valleys.

There weren't many people on the platform but we noticed that a man and his wife and three children kept looking at us. We must have been a strange sight: I was wearing a collarless shirt with a brightly coloured scarf, cut-me-down long trousers, an oversized jacket, big boots and an old trilby hat. Sylvy looked lovely, her long auburn hair had been oiled and taken in a long coil wound round her head. She wore a colourful, gathered ankle-length dress with a pinny over the top, high lace-up boots and a shawl over her shoulders. We carried a brown paper carrier bag each and had an old battered, cardboard case secured by a leather belt.

With a lot of huffing and puffing of smoke and hissing of steam the train pulled in to the station. Jumping on quickly, we found a compartment to ourselves but were disappointed when the man from the station with his wife and children came and sat with us. After they'd all settled down, he smiled at us and said 'Hello'. We answered politely. One of their children was a girl about ten, another a boy of around seven and there was a babe in arms. The man asked us where we were travelling to and were we on our own? I said that Sylvy was with me, my Dad was travelling and my Mom was in hospital and I told him the name of the village in the valleys where we were heading. His wife smiled warmly and said, 'We're going to Porthcawl on our holidays so we'll be travelling as far as Bridgend after changing at Cardiff. Do you mind if we travel with you and at Bridgend we'll make sure you catch the right train?' We thanked them for their kindness. They talked amongst themselves and we spoke to each other in our own language – Romanes. The adults were fascinated and the two children listened open-mouthed. After ten minutes or so they asked us what language we were speaking and where did we come from? Like a lot of Romany children, starting when we were still in the cradle, we were continually being told our history with great pride, so we told them we were Romany Gypsies and that many hundreds of years ago we originally came from India. We told them where we lived and the sort of life we led. During the journey we even tried to teach the children some Romany words.

Then the boy said he was hungry so packets of sandwiches and cakes were brought out of their bag and offered to us as well. We both refused – we would never accept food from a *gorgio* – saying we would shortly be eating our own food. Seeing them eating made us hungry: we laid several large, spotlessly clean cloths across our knees and over part of the seat, we wiped our hands with a damp cloth, then we took out a large homemade loaf, a big piece of cheese and an onion, plus a piece of beef. With a very sharp knife I cut off several thumbs of bread, cheese, onions and beef and placed them on one of the cloths for Sylvy, then did the same for myself. To drink we each had a bottle of cold, sweet, milky tea. The man said, 'Good God, that food looks and smells better than ours.' His family nodded their agreement and it wasn't long before everyone was eating some of our food.

We talked all the way to Bridgend, which made the journey seem shorter. The dad shook our hands, the mother hugged and kissed us. We didn't like this show of affection from a *gorgio,* but we accepted it out of politeness, and the two children waved goodbye as we boarded the train for the final leg. This train stopped at every station and the driver and porters knew everyone boarding and alighting and spent quite a bit of time chatting and laughing before the driver eased the train slowly off along the lines again.

Uncle Stephen was there to greet us, sixty years old, grey, short and stocky and carrying a white stick. He had once worked down the pit until a fall of coal had robbed him of his eyesight some twenty-five years earlier. On hearing our voices he put out his hand and welcomed us to Wales. The first thing he did was touch the top of my head, declaring,

'You've grown at least a foot since I saw you last.' Turning to Sylvy, he asked if he could touch her face, shoulders, arms and hands. When she said 'yes', he gently touched those parts of her body, explaining that that was how he created an image. Clasping her hand with his raw-boned fingers, he looked at the girl and said, 'You're a very pretty young lady and I envy the man you marry.' Sylvy looked at me and blushed with pleasure – Uncle Stephen had made a friend.

Aunty Lizzy was at the cottage door to meet us and fussed about, making sure we would feel at home. Showing us to our rooms, I could see the look of consternation on Sylvy's face: she'd never slept in a house before and was worried she wouldn't be able to breathe, but Lizzy remembered how I had felt on my first visit and put our beds right under the open window with the breeze blowing in.

After a good meal Uncle Stephen took us for a walk up the mountain. Despite being blind, he knew every inch of the way, all the footpaths and nearly every nook and cranny. He told us he not only saw with his ears and hands but with his nose and feet as well. This made us laugh, but then he explained how he could feel the different sorts of surface with his feet and hear the sounds they made as he walked along; also how different smells came to his nose depending on which way the wind was blowing. Sometimes the wind brought mountain smells, at other times the smell of the pit and its workings; sometimes the smell of the fields and yet again the tang of the sea. As he mentioned the sea, he stopped and pointed and said, 'Can you see that silver strip between those two mountains?' When we said, 'Yes', he said, 'That's the sea.' Sylvy's mouth opened in surprise and she whispered to me, 'I thought he couldn't see.' I saw my uncle's mouth twitch in a suppressed smile as he overheard her remark but said nothing. I explained what Aunty Lizzy had told me on a previous visit: how he knew everything there was to know about the mountain, having been brought up here. I said she'd be surprised what Uncle Stephen 'saw'.

During the first two weeks we explored the public footpaths, bridleways and shortcuts, crossed the fields, went up the mountain and along the river banks. Then the Monday morning came when we were supposed to go to school. We weren't used to being enclosed for a large part of the day and we were dreading it. The teacher was a lay preacher called Mr Griffiths, born and bred in the village. He glared at us over the thin-rimmed glasses perched on the end of his red beaky nose, on which there hung a precarious dewdrop. He rubbed his bony hands together, looked at the class of children – all obediently sitting at their desks with their hands resting on top – and said in a strong Welsh lilt, 'My, my, what have we here?'

'Children,' he sang, 'we are greatly honoured today for this boy and girl have come to join us. Aren't we lucky?' The heavy sarcasm was very noticeable in his voice as he continued, 'I think you will all feel the same as I do because they are not *Welsh* like us, they are *English*.' The children laughed at his twisted humour as he went on. 'Children, children,' holding up his hand for silence, 'But, but, children, they are not only *English*. Can you guess what else they are?' The class was silent. 'No? Then I will tell you. They are *Gypsies*.' He spat the last word out as if it was burning his tongue and looked at us with spite and distaste in his eyes. We sat together at a desk that had been moved away from the others. The teacher turned to the class, saying, 'We'd better keep them separated from us, for we don't want to catch anything, do we?' Again all the children shrieked with laughter. Neither of us said a word, we were embarrassed and upset but were determined not to show it. We were used to prejudice and harassment wherever we went.

Mr Griffiths thought he would have some enjoyment at our expense and see how much we knew. He wrote several sums on the board and was surprised to see that Sylvy and I worked them out before most of the class. He tested us on English, History and Geography and was miffed to find we knew nearly all the answers. This was thanks to my Mom, who, when she wasn't away ill, taught us every day, having received a good education herself.

At playtime the girls played in a different playground from the boys but we stood as close as we could by the railings. Some girls came over and asked Sylvy to play. At first she said, 'No thank you,' but I told her to go and make friends. Then the class bully, a big ginger-haired lad called Geraint Lewis who was several inches taller and two stone heavier than anyone else, moved towards me, backed up by his weakling supporters. As he came closer he hissed, 'You're a dirty, stinking Gyppo and we don't want you here!' Just as we squared up to each other, moving round like two fighting cocks, the bell rang for the end of playtime and the teachers came out to keep order as we returned to class. 'We'll get you after school,' the bully boy muttered.

At the end of afternoon school there was a mob of children hanging around by the gates waiting for us to go out. I was worried about Sylvy, so we walked close to a teacher who was going past Uncle Stephen's house and that thwarted the bully's intentions.

Uncle Stephen and Aunty Lizzy wanted to know how we'd got on. Sylvy told them she had made some friends and how nice the girls were. I didn't say much, only that I didn't like the teacher. After tea the two of us went down by the river and sat on the bank in the sun talking about home. As long as we had each other we would be all right, we said. Both of us were homesick. On the way back to the cottage we were confronted by 'Ginger' and about eight other children, who suddenly came out of a gap in the hedge. Without any warning, Lewis ran at me and, catching me completely off-guard, hit me as hard as he could in the face, knocking me down to the ground. Then he kicked me in the stomach, chest and on the side of my head. Sylvy, like a wildcat, leapt on his back and clawed her nails across his cheeks, leaving deep, bloody gouges. But she was no match for the boy: he flung her off and punched her in the face, knocking her into the hedge. I was winded and there was nothing I could do to protect her. The children ran away laughing as the bully-boy shouted, 'There's a lot more of that if you stay around here.'

When I got my breath back I comforted Sylvy, who had a bloody nose and a big red mark on her cheek. She was crying because of the state of my face. Aunty Lizzy nearly fainted when she saw us and she told Uncle Stephen to fetch the policeman. Things looked a little better when our faces had been washed. I'd got a closed black eye, a swollen, cut nose and a big bruise on the side of my head. The bruises on my chest and stomach showed later. No matter what my Aunty and Uncle said, I was determined to settle the score the Romany way – I would avenge the attack, and no *gavver* would be involved.

PC Thomas Vaughan, the village bobby (known as the Gentle Giant and a great friend of my Uncle's), arrived and after settling us down tried to get us to tell him who had carried out the attack. I told him we were of Romany blood and would look after it ourselves. No amount of persuasion, cajoling or veiled threats about taking the law into our own hands had any effect, we stubbornly refused to say anything. PC Vaughan asked Uncle Steve to pass on any information but Uncle replied, 'They won't say anything, that's the way they are. He's a chip off the old block, his Dad was a champion fighter and he's trained all his sons to fight. He reckons this one could be a future champion. He's strong, fast and, according to his Dad, punches above his weight.' This troubled the policeman even more as he realised I could get into serious trouble, especially as there was a strong prejudice in the area against Gypsies.

The following morning we insisted on going to school despite Aunty Lizzy's protestations. All eyes turned towards us as we entered the classroom, the sneering teacher took one look at us and spat, 'You pair of animals have been fighting each other, I suppose?'

'That's the sort of bigoted remark we can do without, thank you, Mr Griffiths.' The teacher looked startled and whirled round to see PC Vaughan standing behind him. 'After I've spoken to the children, perhaps you will come with me to see the headmaster.' Mr Griffiths blanched but said nothing.

The policeman addressed the class of silent children; several of the gang looked uncomfortable. 'Last evening a very serious assault took place on George and Sylvy. It was a completely unprovoked and cowardly attack perpetrated by bullies and cowards. So far George and Sylvy will not say who it was – this is misguided and I *will* get to know who the culprits are. When I do they'll be charged with a serious offence and if I have anything to do with it they'll be sent away from home for a very long time. I'm ashamed that we can't welcome two newcomers to the valley. Just because they've been brought up differently from you and me, it's no excuse to do them any harm. Perhaps your teacher will tell you that it isn't very long ago we fought a war to stop this sort of thing happening.' He went on, 'I'm going to give the ones who did this a chance to admit it and if they do I'll make sure the court knows they owned up. That will go in their favour – or if you know who did it, come and tell me or the headmaster. We won't say who gave us the information.'

Mr Griffiths was severely reprimanded by the headmaster for his obvious bigotry and warned as to his future conduct – which further increased his dislike for us. We were interviewed by the headmaster, Mr Williams, but still wouldn't say who had attacked us.

Our wounds healed in the course of the next few days and two of the gang said sorry. Lewis kept his distance, always sending one of his cronies to find out where we were before coming into the playground or making his way home. I'd sent word to him that I was angry, *very* angry, not particularly about what he had done to me but over what he had done to Sylvy. I was upset that I hadn't been able to do anything to prevent it and I felt I had let her down. I was going to make him pay for everything – when an opportunity presented itself.

We both joined the local sports club where PC Vaughan taught boxing and self-defence (at which I became his star pupil). I also played rugby for the under-fifteens. Sylvy, although small, found she was good at netball and quickly became established as the team shooter due to her uncanny ability to 'find the net'. She was popular with the girls at school because she'd told them she was going to marry me on our sixteenth birthday – how her Dad had promised my Dad, when we were only one day old, that she was mine if I wanted her when we grew up and how the family were making a new wagon for us to live in. The girls thought this was romantic and wished it was them.

Geraint Lewis – Ginger – was one of the best boxers in the club. Unfortunately he used his skill to bully and had been threatened with expulsion on several occasions. I was still waiting to take my revenge when a club boxing contest was announced. Lewis put his name down, confident he would win his division again. Despite me being one and a half stone lighter and two inches shorter than Lewis, I persuaded Mr Vaughan to put me in the same weight class. He didn't know but strongly suspected the reason and he agreed. Dad, a former champion fighter, had taught me how to fight bare-fist and how to box with gloves on. He'd concentrated on a good defence and I'd developed a strong left jab followed by a hard right uppercut. 'Try and find your opponent's weakness if you can,' he'd say, 'and when you've found it, exploit it, turn it to your advantage. Undermine their confidence, keep jabbing away.'

The Division was split into two sections. Mr Vaughan made sure Lewis was in the other section from me so we wouldn't meet in the preliminary rounds. He was strong and skilful and usually won all his fights. I watched his contests, looking for a weakness. He was good but on occasions I saw him wince and hold on after a hard body blow – so that's what I concentrated on in training. My aim was to humiliate him – I needed to beat him convincingly. I was determined I would succeed, I would not countenance failure: he would be paid back for what he'd done to Sylvy. We both progressed through the preliminary rounds and I was excited and determined to win when I realised we were to meet in the final.

On the night of the finals nearly all the village plus many people from the surrounding villages filled the hall to capacity. I refused to shake hands and in the end the referee, a colleague of Mr Vaughan, held my wrist and pushed my glove against Lewis's. At the bell we circled warily, jabbing and feinting without a great deal of action taking place. When the bell went for the second round I did what my Uncle Reuben had taught me – I anticipated the start of the round and was off my stool like a scalded cat. I caught the bully-boy off guard as he was ponderously getting off his stool. I feinted with a high left hand which he followed and then I sank one of the hardest punches I'd ever released with my right hand deep into his solar plexus. I knew it was a winner as I felt the expulsion of air blow onto my face. I quickly pushed my opponent onto the ropes and unleashed a flurry of blows into his unprotected face. His arms fell loosely to his sides, his mouth was agape and his eyes staring blankly, but I wouldn't let him fall. I was still lashing piston-like accurate punches onto his head when the referee dragged me off. Lewis fell flat onto the canvas, further injuring his face. There was no need to count, he was out cold. The doctor rushed into the ring to attend to the unconscious boy who was later taken to hospital. My hand was raised in victory and later I was presented with the champion's cup, which I accepted on behalf of Sylvy. Revenge was certainly sweet.

Later, PC Vaughan asked me if it was Lewis who had attacked us – I said yes it was but that, as far as I was concerned, it was over. He said, 'It's not over for me. I'm going to have a word with him and caution him as to his future behaviour. I'm not going to say you said anything, I'll tell him I found out. He can't be allowed to get away with it.'

The policeman was as good as his word and it was noticeable that Ginger Lewis's behaviour improved and the bullying stopped. We'll never know whether it was down to the warning from the police or the fact he had been beaten in the ring.

Sylvy was out of the valley playing netball for the school and I was at a loose end when I happened upon Dewi Ellis sitting on the river bank. When he saw me he put his finger across his lips to tell me to keep quiet. I sat beside him and he nodded towards the river. I looked where he had indicated and there was a shoal of good-sized trout. He didn't say anything for a while, then he said, 'By reading the river bank, you can work out probable places some of those fish may be tonight, so I'll be back later to see if I can catch any.'

'How are you going to do that?' I asked. Annoyingly, he did what my Uncle Reuben used to do when he didn't want to tell anybody anything; he tapped the side of his nose. In other words, 'Mind your own'. I found out the next day he'd been back and caught a couple of decent trout by tickling them.

I felt sorry for Dewi. He was the eldest of a large family of Welsh Travellers who lived in two static wagons and a dilapidated cottage on a deserted farmstead half-way up a mountain. They rarely mixed with the villagers but kept themselves to themselves. Dewi's dad had been severely crippled in a trotting-horse race. Both his legs had been broken and set so badly they were now twisted; he couldn't stand without a support and could only shuffle a few paces with the aid of two crutches. He was unable to work but spent his time fashioning and decorating model *vardos* and carts which Dewi would sell at fairs. But the main onus for supporting the family fell on Dewi, who would push or pull a large handmade cart – he couldn't afford a horse – all around the valleys, collecting scrap. Anything that was useful was put on one side. The rest was collected once a year by a lorry from a scrap merchant's in Bridgend. Old bikes were cannibalised to make complete ones which were cleaned up, painted and sold; the same with toys and anything else that could be made serviceable (it's the Romany's boast that money can be made out of things discarded by a *gorgio*).

Dewi's mom, who was continually pregnant, nearly always presented a cheerful face to the world, but at times she appeared to be looking into the distance, lost in her own thoughts, perhaps thinking of what might have been. The conditions the family lived in were awful; everything was old and falling to pieces and there were many leaks where the rain trickled in, making all their belongings damp. The children had hacking coughs and wheezy chests. Mrs Ellis did her best to make things comfortable; her brood were clean and tidy but with threadbare clothes and quite often running around barefooted. The living area was spotless but at times, Dewi said, his mom would be found crying at the sheer hopelessness of the situation. Dewi confided in me that once he had found his mom up the top of the mountain, standing on the edge of a steep cliff and looking down into the valley below. He said he sidled up to her, put his arm round her and told her that they couldn't do without her, they all loved her. She wrapped her arms tightly round him and said, 'Oh Dewi, when I had you fifteen years ago I didn't expect to have a new baby nearly every year. Now I'm having another.'

Dewi, who had been seeing to the needs of some of the village girls for a while and knew all about the facts of life, took the unusual step (amongst our people such things would never be spoken about by mother and son) of trying to tell her there were steps that could be taken to avoid her having so many babies, but she wouldn't listen. He told me all she said was, 'A man has his rights' and, so saying, gave Dewi a kiss on the cheek and went back down the mountain. Despite all his problems, he had an effervescent spirit – it was like trying to push a cork underwater; at times he was *too* cheerful!

Once, I'd arranged to go with him to try and catch a few pheasants and he talked non-stop, didn't listen to what I was saying and was all of a twitch. I looked at his eyes and saw that his pupils were as big as saucers – a sign that he'd been drinking or had taken something (this had been explained to me once by Uncle Reuben when we'd found one of my cousins acting very strangely). Dewi denied it and laughed. I refused to go hunting with him and advised him not to go either. He took no notice and wandered off into the woods. Several days later I saw him again and he said he was sorry; he wouldn't use it again as he had nearly been caught, just avoiding capture by swimming across the river. He told me the name of a hedgerow vine whose leaves could be smoked if you dried them and they would help you forget all your troubles. I pointed out to him the effect it would have on his family should he be sent to prison (which I thought at the time was a real possibility), and he agreed with me.

Dewi and I showed each other different ways of catching fish, eels and pheasants, but one of the most important things I taught him was how to listen. I passed on what Grandad and my Dad had shown me. Quite often Grandad used to say, 'I'm going deaf so you'll have to be my ears and listen for me.' And later on Dad said the same thing. Wherever we were, Dewi and me would stop and I would say, 'What can you hear?' Dewi would reel off all the different sounds he could hear and I would do the same – generally I could hear more than he could and he wanted to know how. I would tell him a specific sound he wasn't able to hear, I would describe the sound to him, turn him to face the direction it was coming from, cup both his hands behind his ears, try and blot out any other sounds and really concentrate on the one I had told him about. After a lot of practice he could hear what I was able to hear. No matter where we were, we always practiced picking up sounds. If you go poaching, as well as a good pair of eyes you need a keen pair of ears!

On one of Dad's irregular visits to the valleys to see how Sylvy and me were getting on, I asked him if he would come with me to meet the Ellis family to see if there was anything he could do to help them. On this occasion Uncle Reuben had come down with Dad and he came with us to see Dewi's mom and dad as well. I'd asked Mr and Mrs Ellis and they'd said Dad and anybody else would be welcome. Dad, Uncle Reuben, Sylvy and me were duly making our way up the mountain when Dad paused and we all stopped. Sylvy and I knew we were going to be asked the same question we were asked every time Dad or Uncle Sam (Sylvy's dad) came to see us: 'Don't you think it's time you came back?' When Dad had moved out of earshot again, Reuben told us Dad was going to say that we couldn't stay here much longer and there was going to be a discussion with Uncle Steve and Aunty Lizzy. Sitting on a grassy slope, Dad now said, 'You two were only supposed to be away for a couple of months at the longest but time has gone on and you've been away for well over a year now. You'll have to come back'. Turning to Sylvy, Dad continued, 'Your Mom needs you to help her and I need George to learn more about the *grys* (horses). I'm going to have a talk with Steve and Lizzy, with you there, and we'll make a decision.'

It wasn't up for discussion – that was what was going to happen, so neither Sylvy nor me said anything. We carried up the mountain. On reaching the Ellises' camp, we were greeted effusively by Mr Ellis while his wife stood in the background with the children. For once Dewi was quiet. Everything was neat, clean and tidy. Dewi had tidied up the outside and the few outbuildings and his mom had done her best with the old cottage and the two wagons. A lovely meal had been prepared by Mrs Ellis and her two eldest daughters: there were several spit-roast pheasants, a *cookerell* of *shushi jogray* (a pot of rabbit stew) and a few trout cooked in a tin covered with embers. Mrs Ellis had also made some bread, and it was all washed down with tea sweetened with condensed milk. Very little was said during the meal and afterwards Dewi's mom, Sylvy and the girls cleared away and washed up. Dewi and me were invited to sit with the men.

Mr Ellis asked his son to show Dad the model wagons and carts he had made. Dad was impressed and, much to Dewi's dad's delight, said he could sell as many as could be supplied at the fairs of Stow-on-the-Wold and Appleby. After negotiating a fair price, he placed a big order and paid in advance. Mr Ellis called his wife over and handed all the money to her, saying, 'Go to town and get new clothes for yourself and all the children.' Poor Mrs Ellis burst out crying.

Reuben chatted to Dewi about the scrap business and was completely taken aback when he saw the size of the cart that Dewi pulled to collect his scrap in. Then we all went to look at the outbuildings which, although neglected, were basically sound. Dad asked how long the family had lived up on the mountain and was told sixteen years. He also wondered whether they had been approached by the owners or asked to pay any rent – to both of which questions the answer was 'No'. They believed that, following the death of the old lady who used to live at the farm, the family who it belonged to had died out and due to its isolated position and barren land nobody was interested in buying or renting it.

Before leaving, Dad arranged to take Mrs Ellis to the *borogav* (big town) the following morning. We said our farewells and on the way back down to the valley Sylvy and me were told to walk ahead whilst the two men talked about how they could help the Ellises. The next day Reuben put a proposal to Mr Ellis and Dewi. He said he would go into the scrap business with Dewi, collecting all the metal Dewi could stockpile (sorted into ferrous and non-ferrous) twice a year and selling it in the Midlands, where the price would be considerably higher than Dewi would get from the local scrap-dealer. Reuben told Dewi he would provide him with a horse and cart to enable him to travel further and to increase the volume of scrap he could collect. Also, he would buy a trap for the family to use when Dewi didn't need the horse. Everything was agreed to and sealed by a *vastrisser sar chungra* (handshake with spit). We left the Ellises in a state of great excitement, particularly Dewi because he would no longer have to pull a heavy cart and was now 'in business'. Mr and Mrs Ellis and the children were all looking forward to going out in the horse and trap.

The next day a family meeting took place where everybody could put their point of view without interruption. Up for discussion was whether Sylvy and me should go back with Dad and Uncle Reuben. At a meeting like this a decision was made by a show of hands, unless the *Sherengro* used his position to overrule what had been decided. It was accepted that he had the power to do this – Dad was the *Sherengro*.

Uncle Steve and Aunty Lizzy spoke first. They said that they had really enjoyed having us, we hadn't been a burden, in fact we had been very helpful and they would love us to stay longer. Poor old Aunty Liz became very emotional and said she wished she could adopt us, she loved us so much. Uncle Steve pointed out that we had many friends in the village and that Sylvy was an important member of the netball team whilst I belonged to the boxing club and played rugby. Steve also told Dad that he had been down to the school and talked to nearly all the teachers, including the headmaster, and had been told (much to Dad's astonishment) that I was well-behaved, as was Sylvy, and that we were good students, both of us finishing in the top five in the exams. Uncle did say there was one teacher who hadn't got a good word to say about either of us: Mr Griffiths. 'But,' continued Uncle Steve, 'Griffiths is a bitter, bigoted man who hates the English.'

Sylvy and me were then asked our view and we told Dad we were enjoying mixing with other people, we liked school and we had made a lot of friends, including the village policeman, which brought a look of mock horror to my Dad's face. Dad explained that his biggest worry, should we stay any longer, was that we would move away from our culture and, if we embraced the life of the *gorgio*, we could find we wouldn't be fully accepted by either community: not accepted by the Romanies because we had rejected their culture and not accepted by the *gorgios* because of the inherent mistrust of the Romanies. He then asked Reuben what he thought. So far Reuben had said nothing; now he said he thought we should go back but not immediately. We should be allowed to finish the school term and have time to tell everyone what was happening. It wouldn't be fair to Steve and Lizzy suddenly to lose what had become a big part of their lives, but we should be ready to go home when Dad next came back to Wales, just before Christmas. That would give us two years before we were due to get married, enough time to become fully prepared for independence.

When it was our turn to speak again, Sylvy and me both said we agreed with Uncle Reuben but we asked Dad if it would be possible to carry on going to school? Dad said that he had already thought about it but that during the day we would both be involved in learning other skills to enable us to look after ourselves once we were married. Seeing the disappointment on our faces, he said that if we were serious about carrying on our education he would pay for tutors to teach us in the evenings and at the weekend. We knew it would be hard work but we were both willing to give it a go. Dad then put the first proposal to the meeting: 'Should Sylvy and I return with him and Reuben at the end of the visit?' No hands were raised. He then put the second proposal: that we should return in time for Christmas thus giving us time to prepare? Only Aunty Lizzy didn't raise her hand – she was too busy wiping away her tears. Dad stood up and said 'That's how it will be!'

Later, Sylvy and me were to regret not going back straight away, but you never know what's around the corner. For the time being we were happy to be staying a few months longer.

There was another occasion when I had dealings with Constable Vaughan.

It was the day of the Sunday school walk. Sylvy and me watched the group of walkers start their journey over the mountains to a village in the next valley. Once there, they would hold a joint morning service, enjoy a good lunch, be entertained and then return home over the mountain. The weather was bright and fourteen children aged between ten and fifteen, four teachers and the vicar were all looking forward to the ramble. The route wasn't particularly arduous in the good weather conditions – when you could see the edges of the quarries, avoid the scree slopes and the marshy area, not to mention the myriad illicit mine workings, old and new, where for generations local people had looked for coal.

Mid-morning, we were helping in the garden when Uncle Stephen stood up to stretch his back. Turning to face the wind, he said, 'The wind's changed direction, there's going to be a change in the weather.' Then he added, 'George, keep an eye on the mountain and tell me if you notice any clouds building up low over the peaks.' He went inside to telephone the police station and tell PC Vaughan about his concern.

After lunch we noticed thick cloud bubbling up over the mountain top. I told Uncle and he said, without too much conviction, 'Let's hope it doesn't come right down into the valley. Hopefully the wind will move it.' Within an hour, not only had the mountain disappeared from view but the valley was enveloped in dense cloud, making visibility virtually nil. The fog was mixed up with industrial fumes from the other valleys and it stung your eyes and clogged your nose. Although it was only three o'clock, it seemed like night; nothing was moving, no traffic, no people, and all that could be heard was the occasional muffled thud and the distorted bleating of cattle.

PC Vaughan had groped his way to Uncle's cottage to tell him that the vicar in the other valley had been contacted and had confirmed that the Sunday school party had left over an hour ago. They might well now be stranded on the mountain.

'Right,' said Uncle, 'Let's put the plan into action.'

The three of us went to the stone shed and rechecked all the equipment we might need to effect a rescue. In each pack there were ropes, carefully coiled and snag-free, torches with spare batteries and bulbs, waterproof sheets, blankets, well-stocked first-aid kits, flasks of drinking water, beakers, chocolate bars and mint cake – we added flasks of hot drinks. Carried separately were two collapsible stretchers. We each had a whistle and a klaxon on lanyards round our necks.

Uncle Steve addressed us. 'George, you'll come with me and Tom. Lizzy, you and Sylvy go carefully from door to door and get a team of ladies to go to the hall and prepare hot drinks, soup and bread rolls. Get blankets, towels and stretchers ready. Try and phone the doctor and district nurse and see if you can get them to stand by at the hall.'

'Stephen?' Tom Vaughan queried, 'don't you think George is a bit young?'

'Yes,' snapped Uncle, 'but he's fit and strong and the one thing I've noticed about him is his extraordinary sense of hearing, much better than yours and certainly a lot better than mine. He can pick up sounds I can't hear and he might save valuable time or even prevent us going past the children.'

The policeman agreed. With several other women, Aunty Lizzy and Sylvy made their way to the village hall. Uncle Stephen, PC Vaughan and me started to walk to the mountain, each of us with the large pack on our backs. The higher we got, the denser the fog became.

'I'll go first, Tom. We'll have George in the middle and you follow. Keep as close together as you can and blow your whistle if you're in trouble. When we get higher we'll start sounding the klaxons and listening for a response. We'll do that every hundred yards or so and hopefully they'll hear us if they're sheltering somewhere off the track.'

The cloud became so thick you couldn't see a hand in front of you. We'd sounded the klaxons several times and heard nothing. PC Vaughan was bringing up the rear and was finding it difficult to keep his footing. He kept stumbling as he strayed off the track and at one point he caused Uncle Steve to laugh out loud, much to the policeman's embarrassment. As Tom lay full length on the ground, having tripped over, he shouted in sheer frustration, 'How the bloody hell can you see where you're going, Steve? I can't see a sodding thing!' My uncle stopped, looked down towards the direction of the voice and retorted, 'I can't see *anything*, can I, you silly bugger!' Realising what he had said, PC Vaughan apologised, but the more he tied himself in knots, the more Uncle Steve laughed.

Progress was very slow. Every noise was muffled, everything seemed still and eerie – and soaking wet. We skirted past marshy areas, along the edge of quarries, up steep mountain tracks, pausing, sounding the klaxons and listening. Several times we thought we heard voices, but it turned out to be sounds from the valley below or the bleating of sheep. After two hours of walking, we were passing a lot of old workings when I heard a cry for help. I listened and there it was again. I shouted for Uncle Stephen and Tom Vaughan to stop.

'I've heard someone shouting. It was faint but I definitely heard someone,' I told them.

All three of us listened intently, cupping our ears in the direction of the sound, but nothing was heard.

'Are you sure, George?' queried the policeman.

'Yes.'

We blew the whistles as hard as we could, then sounded the klaxons. 'There it is again,' I cried. 'It's to the left-hand side of the track.'

Uncle Stephen and Tom Vaughan could hear nothing. We tried again after another hundred yards or so and this time we all heard cries for help. Uncle Steve thought for a few seconds and then said, 'I reckon they're sheltering under that big overhang by the old workings. We'll have to be extra careful or we'll finish up in trouble ourselves.'

Every few yards we blew our whistles; the cries were getting nearer and nearer until we could clearly hear a hubbub of voices.

Tom shouted, 'Whatever you do, don't come towards us. We'll come to you.'

'DO NOT MOVE,' shouted Steve.

We rounded a corner and there, huddled under a large overhang, were the Sunday school party – teachers, the vicar and a lot of frightened children. Hugs and handshakes were exchanged and tears of relief flowed. Luckily no one was injured, only cold and wet; soon they were wrapped in poncho-style waterproof blankets, warm hats and gloves, and were munching on chocolate and mint cake and enjoying a warm drink. They had been on the mountain for over four hours and were anxious to start down again. It had taken nearly two hours to find them; now, with small children, it would take at least three to four hours to get back to the village, barring any accidents.

A 'crocodile' was organised with everyone linked to each other by a rope. Each adult was given a whistle on a lanyard to be blown should anyone be in trouble. My uncle would lead, followed by some of the youngest children, then a teacher, then more children followed by another teacher until it got to me and the policeman bringing up the rear. It took over three hours to get back down the mountain and reach the hall where there was a large gathering of people, including the vicar's wife, the children's parents and other relations, Sunday school teachers, the headmaster and his wife and a lot of volunteer helpers. As we entered there was a great big cheer, more hugs and kisses and a lot more tears. The doctor examined everyone including the rescue party and all were passed fit and well. The vicar gave an impromptu service of thanksgiving with all denominations taking part – even the non-believers joined in.

Everyone spent a sleepless night in the hall as the fog was even thicker in the village than up on the mountain, but we were able to return home as the fog cleared and the sun started to shine the following morning. Although we were tired we went to school where, unbeknownst to me, the headmaster had gone into school early to organise a presentation in front of the pupils and teachers. As I walked into the school I was waylaid by Mr Llewellyn the PT teacher, who asked if I would consider entering an inter-schools long-distance running race. He said that it was early days yet and there would be plenty of time to practise and get fit. I was more than a little nonplussed and wondered why he was asking me as I'd never shown any interest in distance running. We were interrupted by another teacher, 'Jock' Minto (a Scot in a Welsh school who taught English), who said to Mr Llewellyn that assembly was about to start. We went into the hall and, much to my embarrassment, everybody stood up and clapped and cheered, after which Mr Williams, the head, told everybody about the mountain rescue and how I had been involved. He then presented me with a book token. The headmaster was a friendly and fair man, though firm and strict when necessary; he made us all laugh when he said he would be in trouble with the school secretary as he had stolen the book token from several that had been purchased as prizes for the high achievers in the end of term exams. The only teacher who didn't shake my hand and say 'Well done' was Mr Griffiths. At playtime I had to recount details of the rescue many times as nearly all the children wanted to hear all about it.

Aunty Lizzy was very proud when a photograph of the rescue party and a full account of what had happened appeared in the local paper.

After the Sunday school rescue Mr Griffiths was even more hostile towards us, being especially nasty to Sylvy. During the last lesson of the next day, as he walked past our desk, he sniffed the air, went past us, then turned back and stood next to us. He looked at the class and said, 'Can anybody else detect an offensive smell?' No one answered; most of the pupils looked down at their desks. He went back to the front of the class and continued, 'If you can't, you must all have bad colds because I can certainly smell something. Come out here,' he said to me. I went up to the front and he sniffed again. 'Sit down, it's not you. Come out here,' he now said to Sylvy, who went up in turn. 'Don't come any closer. I can tell it's you. When did you last change your clothes and have a wash? It can't have been lately because you smell.'

He turned to the rest of the class and said, 'You must have noticed that Gypsies smell, especially English Gypsies.'

No one sniggered or reacted, they all kept quiet. I clenched my fists but decided I would tell Uncle Steve and he could come with us to see the headmaster. I was ever so upset as Sylvy was very fastidious when it came to personal hygiene.

'Sit down, you smelly girl, and stay behind after class. I need to have a word with you.'

Sylvy was embarrassed and close to tears. I held and squeezed her hand under the desk.

At the end of lessons the teacher told everyone they could go apart from Sylvy. I stayed behind with her but Griffiths ordered me out and told me to wait outside in the playground. I waited for about fifteen to twenty minutes until Sylvy came running out of school all red-faced and tearful. I asked her what the matter was but she didn't answer. She ran past me, making for the cottage. I chased after her but she wouldn't speak.

She charged into the house, nearly knocking over Uncle Steve, went upstairs and bolted the door. We could all hear her sobbing hysterically. She wouldn't undo the door for me or Uncle so Aunty Lizzy told us to go downstairs whilst she tried. I said to Uncle Steve that she had had to see Mr Griffiths after school had ended and I told him what the teacher had said about Sylvy smelling. Uncle was furious and promised to visit the school in the morning. From downstairs we could hear Aunty and Sylvy talking and both were crying. I went up to try to see her but Sylvy screamed at me to go away. I couldn't understand it.

Aunty Liz looked at me and said, 'Leave us alone for a while until Sylvy has calmed down and ask your uncle to come up here please. Steve went upstairs and came back down looking very grave. I asked him to tell me what the matter was but he said, 'Run down to PC Vaughan's and ask him to come up here straight away.'

'Why?' I asked.

'Just do it.'

Within a few minutes the policeman was at the house but when Sylvy saw him she screamed at him to go away. PC Vaughan said, 'I'll be back shortly – I'm going to get some help.' In less than an hour a policewoman in civilian clothes and a female doctor were at the house.

No one would tell me what was going on and I was starting to get angry. The two women went upstairs into Sylvy's room. All I could hear was Sylvy sobbing and saying over and over again, 'He won't want me any more. He won't marry me now.'

The policewoman came downstairs and sat by me. 'We need your help.'

Mr Vaughan sat the other side of me and asked me to promise not to do anything silly as this was a police matter and I could get myself into serious trouble.

'What are you are talking about? I don't understand!' I shouted.

WPC Godfrey took me by the hand and said, 'Sylvy says she was assaulted by Mr Griffiths but she won't let us examine her. She's terrified you will no longer marry her. We want you to go up and see her and tell her you still want to marry her and that she must let us examine her. Will you do that? We'll tell you more once we've had a good talk to her and examined her. Okay?'

I nodded and went up to Sylvy's room where she was still crying. Aunty left us alone. Sylvy cowered away from me but I said to her, 'No matter what has happened, no matter what that *bostaris* (bastard) Griffiths has done, I still want to marry you and I will marry you. Nothing will stop me from marrying you.'

'Do you really mean that?'

'Yes I do, *aprey mi Daia's jivaben* (On my mother's life).' I gently cuddled her and kissed her forehead. 'You must show the policewoman and the doctor and tell them everything,' I told her.

She stopped sobbing, the two women came into the room and I went out. After about three quarters of an hour Sylvy and the two ladies came downstairs. Sylvy went with Aunty Lizzy into the front room, Uncle Steve, PC Vaughan, WPC Godfrey and the doctor all went into the kitchen. I stood outside the door to listen.

WPC Godfrey started to talk. 'Sylvy says she was asked to stay and see Mr Griffiths after school. She says,' continued the policewoman, 'that Mr Griffiths pulled down the blind on the classroom door and locked the door. He called her over to him and when she was close enough he grabbed hold of her, dragged her over his knee, pulled her pants down and hit her several times with the flat of his hand on her bare bottom. After he had done that, he asked her if it had hurt, to which Sylvy replied that it had, so he said he had better kiss it better. Then he kissed her on the bottom several times.'

I was terribly shocked when I heard this.

The doctor then took over: 'There are six big bruises on Sylvy's bottom. Part of the bruising is heavier than the surrounding areas, which may have been caused by a ring. There are also some minor abrasions which could have been caused by fingernails. There is no doubt she has been indecently assaulted.'

WPC Godfrey said, 'After the incident had taken place, Sylvy told Griffiths she would report him and he laughed. He said that he was a preacher and a school teacher and had lived all his life in the village and that no one would believe a smelly Gypsy girl because everyone knows all Gypsies tell lies.

Apparently he told her that it was her fault. He called her a "dirty-minded girl" and said it was all her fault: she had made him do it. He said that no one would believe her if she told. Then he shouted at her to get out. You all know the rest.'

I couldn't contain myself any longer and shouted, 'The dirty filthy bastard!' Of course they all realised then that I had been eavesdropping. Uncle Steve opened the door and I was allowed to join them in the kitchen.

Mr Vaughan looked at me and said sternly, 'If you should attempt to take the law into your own hands, you'll not only find yourself in deep trouble, you'll completely jeopardise the case against Griffiths and he'll go scot-free. You must let the police to do their job. It may be a slow process but it will be thorough. So promise me and your Aunty and Uncle you'll do nothing.'

I promised.

As PC Vaughan and WPC Godfrey went down the path, I heard Mr Vaughan say, 'In my own mind I'm confident she's telling the truth, but at the moment it's her word against his. We'll have to tread carefully, this could stir up a lot of bad feelings.'

He was right, it did: the village became divided. Griffiths was arrested on suspicion of indecent assault and taken to the police station where, PC Vaughan told us, he denied any involvement and suggested that it was either me or possibly Uncle Steve who had slapped Sylvy. After his interview he was released on police bail, pending further enquiries. The members of the chapel where he preached were vociferous in their condemnation of Sylvy, who, in their words, was a lying Gypsy slut, and a lot of ill feeling was generated towards Gypsies in general. Even the Ellises, who kept themselves apart from the villagers, were vilified by a section of the community. Mrs Griffiths came to the cottage, shouting and bawling and demanding that Sylvy withdraw the accusation. She received short shrift from Aunty Liz and was quickly sent packing.

Sylvy and me stayed away from school, despite a visit from the headteacher, who urged us to go back. Mr Griffiths had been suspended until this whole unsavoury matter had been resolved.

PC Vaughan sent a message to Dad via the local police. Dad was told the whole story and within a few days he and Uncle Reuben, George, Sylvy's Dad Sam and two of her older brothers had arrived and were camped near the village. Dad promised PC Vaughan they wouldn't cause any trouble but he also said they wouldn't back away from it. Things had reached stalemate, the enquiry had stalled: although there was a lot of circumstantial evidence building up against the teacher, nothing could be positively proved. He had long thin bony fingers – the bruises were long and thin. Some of the bruises showed a heavier mark as if caused by a ring and Mr Vaughan had told Uncle Steve that when he interviewed Griffiths he had a white mark on his wedding finger where a ring had been removed. The teacher said he hadn't been wearing it, including on the day of the alleged offence, as he had a slight infection under the ring. Nothing could be proved.

Sylvy was getting more and more upset as she thought no one believed her, but then there was an unexpected development. A former teacher at the village school, a Mrs Coulson, went to see PC Vaughan, he told us, and informed him that about eight years ago she had been to see Mr Griffiths after school to find his classroom door locked and the blind down. Peeping through a narrow gap, she had seen Myfanwy Jones crying whilst her sister was across Mr Griffiths' lap and he was slapping her bare bottom. Mrs Coulson hadn't said anything before because she was frightened of Griffiths, who was a bully. The village policeman passed the information to CID, who discreetly interviewed the Jones sisters. With a bit of gentle persuasion they agreed to give evidence in court. The news soon went round the village and it wasn't long before several other ex-pupils, the eldest now in her forties, also came forward to say they had been assaulted by Mr Griffiths.

Faced with this overwhelming evidence against him, Griffiths confessed and asked for a lot of other indecency offences to be taken into consideration. Shortly before his trial was to begin, a young chapel Sunday school teacher came forward to allege that Griffiths had committed a very serious offence against her to which he also confessed. It was unnecessary for any of the victims to attend court as Griffiths pleaded guilty to eight charges of indecent assault and a charge of rape against the Sunday school teacher. He was sentenced to six and a half years in jail.

Uncle Reuben, Uncle George and Sylvy's brothers returned home whilst my Dad and Sylvy's dad stayed behind to buy some Welsh cobs. As there were only a few weeks until the end of term they were going to wait and take us back home with them. George and Reuben had left two fully repaired and fully functional trailers that they had towed down. These were delivered to the Ellises by Dad and Uncle Sam to replace their old leaky ones. Dad told us that the whole family, including Dewi, burst into tears when they were told it was a gift 'from one brother to another'.

Sylvy and I returned to school but everything had become tainted and all we wanted to do was go home. But we decided for Uncle Steve and Aunty Lizzy's sake to wait till the end of term. The teachers and all the pupils were really kind to Sylvy and whenever they could they included her in every activity. The headmaster personally apologised to Sylvy and to all the other unfortunate victims of Mr Griffiths at an assembly – this gesture was truly appreciated. At the end of the school term we went round everybody we knew and said our goodbyes. I told Dewi I would travel down with Uncle Reuben when he came to collect the scrap and we would see if we could catch some more pheasants. Dewi shook me by the hand and then quickly disappeared inside his trailer.

We had been away for nearly two years and were sad to be leaving our many Welsh friends, especially Uncle Steve and Aunty Lizzy who we had come to love. On the day we left Uncle was trying hard to be matter-of-fact and casual but he was unable to hide his true feelings. He hugged us and told us how much he had enjoyed having us and hoped we would come down and see them again. Aunty Lizzy wept openly but they both cheered up when Dad told them they were invited to our wedding and he would make all the travel arrangements.

Dad drove us home in his Bedford TK lorry, towing a brand new fully chromed trailer that he had just bought and which was absolutely luxurious inside. We were happy and looking forward to seeing our families. Chatting away, the miles were quickly eaten up. We had passed Abergavenny and were heading towards Herefordshire when we were pulled over by a police patrol car. Two policemen ordered us out and said they wanted to search the lorry and trailer. Dad challenged them, saying they needed a warrant as the trailer was classed as a house. One of them said they did not as they suspected there were stolen goods inside. Our dads accompanied the officers during their search to make sure nothing was planted: finding nothing, they reluctantly gave up.

Whilst they were talking to Dad at the rear of the trailer, Sam noticed that someone had flytipped some builder's rubbish at the side of the road. He picked out a short piece of timber with two large protruding nails and wedged it under the front nearside wheel of the police car. When we finally pulled out and continued on our journey, the police followed us for a few yards then stopped. The men got out, inspected the now flat front tyre, kicked it in frustration and waved their fists at us. We all had a good laugh, crossed over the county boundary into another police area and made our way home.

A big celebration had been laid on for our homecoming that lasted for many hours. All the Tribes, including a lot of Mom's Irish relations, were there. Big fires were lit, lots of food prepared and there was plenty of beer and cider. It wasn't long before everyone was singing, dancing, eating, drinking, laughing and making what you might describe as 'one unholy row'.

Late in the evening things calmed down. Everyone sat around the fire listening to Sylvy's and my adventures, after which some of the old folks, as is traditional, told stories of the old days (all of which had been heard before, but everyone listened respectfully). In the early hours of the morning only a few were left round the embers, with one or two men asleep on the dewy grass, oblivious to the cold.

As I passed Gran's wagon I could see and hear her talking to Sylvy about what her duties would be when she became a wife. I heard Gran say that things were getting a little better than when she first got married. She explained to Sylvy that in her day the woman was the chattel of the man and she was expected to do as she was told, when she was told, without question. She explained how her sister Thurza had been expected to wash her husband's hands and face, comb his hair and help to dress him.

One tradition that was still kept to, Gran said, was that a woman is not allowed to walk in front of a group of men who are talking – when Sylvy was married, if she was chatting to her husband and another man came to talk to her man, she would have to move away and allow the men to talk in private. Also, women are not allowed to discuss 'women's problems' in front of men; they must be discussed out of their earshot. Gran also reminded Sylvy of the strict dress code for Romany women: she must not expose any part of her body and, when sitting, her legs must be closed together with nothing showing. Nor is she permitted to step over food as this would contaminate it.

Gran went on to tell her about her not being able to prepare or handle food during her 'time of the month' and how it wasn't all that long ago that women had had to spend their period time in a separate dwelling. Sylvy was also told that for several weeks after giving birth she would be considered unclean and wouldn't be able to share a bed with her husband. Then there was also the procedure for washing the body and clothes. Our trailers, just like the wooden *vardos*, have no washing facilities, so everything is done using two large stainless steel bowls, one slightly bigger than the other. The smaller bowl is used for preparing vegetables and washing the crocks and tea towels; the bigger one is for washing the family's bodies and clothes – the bowls must never be mixed up. Gran said that some men insisted on having a separate bowl to wash their bodies as they wouldn't use a bowl a woman had used. By tradition, the women would wash the children's clothes first, followed by their own, and lastly the men's clothes. However, the bowl had first to be cleansed with boiling water so the men's garments wouldn't be contaminated by the women's. Sylvy knew all this already but listened to what Gran said respectfully and politely.

Gran loved Sylvy. She stretched out a hand and stroked her arm. 'I know you'll make George a good wife and I know you love each other very much, but you do realise there's one custom that must be kept?' Before Sylvy could answer, Gran went on, 'The morning after your wedding night your sheet must be displayed to show that you were a virgin. Should there be no blood your relationship with the Tribe could be at risk.' Gran held up her hand, silencing Sylvy, and continued talking to the blushing girl. 'You and George have been together for a long time now and feelings run high. Sometimes they're uncontrollable. Me and my Thomas did not have a long courtship but it was very passionate and I expect you and George, like me and Tom, went somewhere quiet and you found yourself lying in the shade while the sun shone on his back. 'Tis natural, so if that's the case, take a sharp *kuri* (knife), make a small cut at the end of one of his toes – don't cut your own, it's him that's caused the trouble so let him suffer a bit – and smear a small amount of blood where you've been lying.' Gran chuckled, 'That's what me and my Tom did.'

Sylvy gave the old woman a *choom* (kiss) and said, 'I love you, Gran,' to which Gran replied, 'And I love you, dearie.'

After we had returned from Wales, the weeks and months seemed to pass slowly but suddenly over a year had passed and there was less than twelve months before we were due to be married on our shared sixteenth birthday. Then, one day Sylvy said, 'I don't want to get married in January, it's cold. If you agree, and only if you agree, let's get married in the May when it's warm. We can have a big gathering outside. We've waited sixteen years, surely another few months won't make much difference? What do you think?'

But I'd only heard part of what Sylvy had said. All I'd heard was, 'I don't want to get married,' before the rest became a blur. My mind had closed and I felt sick. When she saw my face and how pale I was, she stared at me in alarm.

'Sorry, say it all again. I don't understand,' I said.

She repeated what she had said and I could have cried with relief. I shouted, 'If you want to get married in May we'll be married in May! If you want to run away now, we will! If you want me to take you to the moon, I will...'

'Shush, shush, whatever's the matter?' said the astonished girl. I explained that I'd thought she didn't want to get married.

'You silly boy!' She flung her arms around me and we cuddled each other. It wasn't long before, as Gran put it, she was 'lying in the shade'. She had her eyes closed. As I lay looking at her I realised that – although she was only fifteen – the girl had changed into a woman. She was small and slight but she had the figure of a woman many years older. With her big brown eyes, deep auburn hair, freckled nose and a smile that radiated warmth and kindness, she was beautiful and I loved her.

All the women were getting excited about the forthcoming wedding. Sylvy had explained why she wanted to get married in May instead of during the cold month of January and everyone agreed. It was going to be a great affair. Although there were six months to go, verbal invitations had been issued to give the Tribes time to make their arrangements. There was going to be a church wedding, then a traditional Romany one, followed by a massive celebration. Our new wagon, which was to be our home, was finished and we would be spending our first night as man and wife in it. Then we were going to travel on our own to the Judge's Field, the small field in the Peak District given to us by Mr Harrison.

In the September before our sixteenth birthday the following January, Gran sought out Dad and told him to persuade us to get married as first arranged and not postpone it till May. She looked and sounded concerned but wouldn't say why. We went to see her but she just repeated what she had said previously. Eventually Dad got her to tell him what she had seen. She had been looking into her crystal ball and a blurred image of six black horses had come into view; then they disappeared, to be followed by an image of a wagon with a single person in it moving away in the opposite direction from the black horses. Dad pressed her to tell him what she thought it meant but she just said, 'I only saw it for a few moments and I can't get it back. I think it's to do with the young 'uns. Something ain't right. Tell them to get married in January and everything should be all right – tell them to listen to Old Louie. I don't know what it is but I'm worried for them.'

Dad told us what had been said and Sylvy and I agreed that if Gran saw the image again we would change back to January. Gran seemed satisfied, but she didn't see it again. The wedding would be in May. We all had a lovely Christmas, although the weather closed in and January started off wet. Halfway through the month the weather turned to snow and ice and became bitter cold. We cast further and further afield to get fuel for the fires and it was a full-time job breaking ice to water the animals.

Dad had got a small three-year-old horse, just a little bit bigger than a pony, a white-and-black-spotted piebald, suitable for Sylvy to ride. Being small, she looked like a 'Tom-tit on a large round of beef' when she was on a big horse. I wanted it for Sylvy's birthday and Dad said he'd give it to me, but I insisted on paying him a fair price. Deal done, we both spat on one of our hands, as tradition demands, and clapped them together.

On the day of our birthday Sylvy gave me a new *putsi kuri* (pocket knife) and two beautifully balanced *wusting kuris* (throwing knives). When I gave her the little horse her eyes lit up with pleasure and she grinned from ear to ear. She flung her arms round me and gave me a great big kiss. 'Let's go for a ride.' But I said I had to help Dad feeding and watering the animals. 'Okay, I'll go and show Mom and Dad. I'll probably go down the lanes a bit later. Don't worry, I'll be careful,' she said.

I went off up the fields and Sylvy went to see her mom and dad. Later that day she put a halter onto her new horse and, riding bareback, took it down the lane. She had only been gone a few minutes when Gran hurried from her wagon as fast as she could and made her way to Milletti and Sam's wagon. When she got there she called to them, 'Where's the little girl? Don't let her take the horse.'

Sylvy's parents came out to see Gran. 'What's the matter, Louie?' Milletti asked.

'I've seen a *boz* (crow), I've seen a *boz*. Get her back.' Gran was very agitated.

'Where did you see the crow, Louie?' Sam asked her. By this time Gran was near hysterical and incoherent. The parents took the old lady into their wagon and gave her a drink of plum brandy. She eventually calmed down and said, 'A crow's a sign of bad luck, sometimes death. I saw it in the crystal ball.'

Sam said, 'She's only taken her new horse for a little ride. She'll be back very shortly. You stay with us and have something to eat and, you'll see, everything will be all right.'

Gran was still agitated and wouldn't settle. She kept saying over and over again, '*Dordi, dordi* (Oh dear, oh dear). My poor little girl. What will my George do?' She was crying and becoming hysterical again. This alarmed Sam and Milletti so Sam said, 'I'm going to look for Sylvy. Send one of the boys up to Tom and George and tell them what Louie's said.'

As he went out of the wagon the little piebald horse trotted back into the camp without Sylvy on its back.

'Oh God, no, no, no,' shouted Sam.

One of the boys leapt onto the horse and galloped up the fields to tell me and Dad. I nearly passed out when I heard what Gran had said and that the horse had come back by itself. A party of men was quickly organised and we all set off in different directions. I went one way along the towpath, Dad and Sam went in the other direction. After going a couple of miles I called at the lock-keeper's cottage.

'No, no one has been past all day. I haven't seen young Sylvy. She's definitely not been past here, cos I've been doing a bit of hedge-laying and I would have seen her,' he told me.

I thanked him and set off back to find Dad and Sam with panic welling up inside me. I called back at the camp – she still hadn't come back so I returned to the canal and went in the other direction. I'd gone for about a mile when I turned a bend. I could see Dad and Sam kneeling down on the towpath and realised at once they were trying to pump canal water out of Sylvy. I screamed at the top of my voice and ran to where they were. Sam was crying and Dad looked at me, shook his head and said, 'Sorry, my son, we couldn't save her.'

I stared in disbelief at the poor, pathetic, bedraggled little body lying on the ground. She had a cut on her forehead and was covered in grime and weed from out of the canal. We tried again to revive her but all in vain. The three of us were crying and the tears ran off the end of my chin. I picked the little bundle up into my arms, kissed her pretty face and carried her back to the camp. By the time we got there the news had travelled ahead of us, carried back by children who had seen what had happened, and everyone was lined up by the gates. Most of the men and children were crying and the women were wailing.

Gran was in full command of herself again by now. She took me by the arm and guided me to her wagon where we lay poor little Sylvy on the bed. On the way she had asked Milletti to bring a full set of dry clothes which she did and then left. Gran asked me to leave but I wouldn't so between us we undressed the body, washed and dried her, and re-dressed Sylvy in the clean clothes. I stared at her, not wanting to believe what I was seeing. She looked so beautiful, it was as if she was sleeping. 'Perhaps she'll wake up in a minute,' I thought.

My head was bursting with unanswerable questions. Why Sylvy? Why did I give her the horse? If I hadn't given it to her, would she still be here now? I was racked with grief and guilt. I buried my head in Gran's lap and cried until I was exhausted.

Knowing our tradition for a quick burial, for once the authorities co-operated and the formalities relating to the sudden death were dealt with speedily. I kept vigil continuously, not leaving her for a moment until she was taken to be buried.

The day of the funeral was cold but crisp and bright. I wasn't really aware of what was going on around me but I realised there were hundreds of people there. I don't remember the service, I don't even remember walking across the boards laid over the grave and casting the earth. All I know is that many people came to speak to me and say how sorry they were, but I ignored everybody. I couldn't speak to them, I didn't want to speak to them. All I wanted was for them all to go away.

We returned to the camp. Sylvy's belongings had been placed in the new wagon which was going to be our home and I set fire to it and watched it burn to ashes. I walked away and went into Gran's *vardo*. She was a strange, cantankerous old besom but she seemed to be the only one who knew what I was going through. I sat on her bed and she cuddled me as if I was a little boy. While she held me, she told me how she had felt when she lost my Grandad and then went on to tell me how, although she had raised eighteen children, she had also lost five more and that she could still see their little faces; when she thought about it, it still hurt.

'Eventually,' she said, 'you will control the hurt and your lovely Sylvy will go from your head and into your heart where she will remain forever.'

I looked at this funny old lady and realised that at one time she had been young like me and had had her share of grief. We cried together. When I awoke the following morning I was lying on her bed and she was sitting on a chair looking into her crystal ball.

I said, 'Gran, I can't stay here. I've got to get away by myself.'

'I know, George. I saw you going away when I saw the six black horses like the ones used to take Sylvy away and I've just seen you going away again. Do what you want to do, but make sure you think of your old Gran. I'll be watching over you.'

I kissed her and went out. I spoke to no one, not even Dad. He watched me gathering things up and knew what was in my mind. He prepared a fairly new wagon for travel, put a good horse in the shafts and tethered two more to the back. Then he loaded up everything I would need, gave me a large wad of money, embraced me and (something unusual for him) kissed me, shook me by the hand and walked off up the fields. Without a word to anyone, I drove out of the camp. The next thing I remember is being on the Judge's Field in Derbyshire.

The days came and went. I did everything mechanically: fed, watered and exercised the animals, wrote out a grocery list and handed it to the shopkeeper when I needed provisions. I spoke not a word to anyone. The dogs caught rabbits most days from out of the woods and these were my main diet, sometimes as a *jogray*, other times roasted over the fire.

Dad, not a man to show his emotions as a rule, told me later that, though he knew I could look after myself physically, he was worried about how I would cope emotionally. At a meeting of the men it was decided that the most likely place I would have headed was the Judge's Field. Gran confidently told Dad that's where I was but to leave me for a while to try and sort things out. According to Dad, she told him, 'Tom, after what that young lad has been through, he will never be the same and you may be upset at what you find.'

After nearly a year, Dad came looking for me. He arrived in his lorry towing a lovely trailer. He greeted me with a great deal of enthusiasm and I could see the disappointment in his face when it wasn't returned. I was pleased to see him, but I just couldn't show it and all the time he was there I didn't speak to him – I couldn't – my brain wouldn't engage in speech.

The end to my self-imposed mutism came abruptly and violently. It was the day after my birthday, which was also the anniversary of Sylvy's death, and everything was emotionally raw. A young policeman came into the field, pushing his bike. You could feel the tension immediately: he looked nervous and uncertain. We looked at him without speaking. Dad's advice about the *gavvers* was always to let them open up the conversation and see what they'd got on their mind; never volunteer any information first. The constable greeted us and we gave him a curt nod. Then he said, 'There was a series of break-ins last night, the other side of town. Can you account for your whereabouts?' I could feel the bile rising inside me.

Dad replied, 'We were both here.'

'Can anyone else corroborate that?'

'No, we can give each other alibis. And before you go any further, I suggest you talk to Judge Harrison and have a look back in your station records,' said Dad. But before anything else could be said I let go such a tirade of abuse that not only was the officer taken aback, Dad was as well and moved quickly between me and the policeman. The grief and shock of the last twelve months, the years of prejudice, harassment and bigotry had come to the fore. I harangued the now-worried policeman for about ten minutes; no one could get a word in. I ranted and raved at him, all the time being held back by Dad. When I ran out of words, I picked up a big branch from the stack of firewood and started to beat the ground with it. Then I ran into the woods, threw myself down on the ground and sobbed uncontrollably.

Dad sat the white-faced young policeman down, made him a cup of strong, sweet tea and told him all about Sylvy and how I hadn't spoken to anyone for over a year. 'One thing,' Dad said wryly. 'Your visit, as unpleasant as it was for you, has got him talking again.'

After the policeman had left, Dad came and found me and took me back to the *vardo* where he calmed me down. Shortly afterwards I started talking as if I had never stopped. A couple of weeks later Dad was preparing to leave when the same policeman came back. He was still wary of me, but he came right up to us, saying, 'We've apprehended three men from the Midlands for the break-ins and they've admitted a string of other offences as well.' He turned to me and said, 'I'm sorry I upset you but I have a duty to try and find out who committed these crimes and I was sent to interview you. No hard feelings?' He held out his hand which I took and shook. 'Okay if I call and see you from time to time?'

'All right' I said.

Dad and the bobby left together, creating an unlikely sight. The PC's bike was fixed to the back of the wagon and he was sitting up at the front with Dad. I never thought I would see the day when that happened.

Over the next few months PC Green and I developed a friendship, to the extent that he brought his wife and we all had a meal together one evening and on several occasions I visited him. During our visits he told me about himself and his family and how much he had enjoyed being in the Royal Air Force Police. He said it had been a difficult choice whether to remain in the RAF or join the civilian police but his new wife wasn't keen on being posted abroad. I didn't want to return to the camp and live with all my relatives – I wanted to break away and do things on my own. I was now seventeen. Soon I would have to do my national service, so I called into an RAF careers centre and signed on for three years.

I should have been wed and starting a family but I wasn't. It was past a year since I had lost Sylvy and it was still raw and painful. I couldn't go back and start again as if nothing had happened. I wouldn't be able to put up with the Elders telling me to start looking for another wife, nodding their heads sagely and saying, 'You cannot live in the past. Yesterday's gone.' Daughters of friends and female cousins would suddenly be invited and we would find ourselves alone – I didn't want that. I wasn't interested and if I was to resist too long I would cause offence, not only to the girls and their parents but also to the older members of the Tribe. I was in a quandary as to what to do. I sat outside my wagon, staring into the fire and allowing my mind to wander and think of the lovely times Sylvy and me had had together.

Lost in thought, I heard Gran's voice calling me as clearly as I could hear the wind: 'George! George! Listen to me.' Startled, I leapt to my feet. Was it my imagination? A trick of the wind? Perhaps. I sat down and there it was again. 'George! George! Are you listening to me?' The dogs moved as close to me as they could, restless and whining.

I answered, 'Yes, Gran.'

Then I heard, 'Come to me before you go away and we lose you.'

'Yes, Gran.'

Early the next morning I was ready to set off. The weather was fine for the whole of the journey back to the camp. I didn't push the horses and kept up an average of between fifteen to twenty miles a day. As I approached my destination I experienced a mixture of pleasure and trepidation. When I dismounted from the wagon there were a lot of relatives, including my Dad and Gran, to meet me. No one asked any questions and, much to my relief, no one mentioned Sylvy. Several of the men went out with their dogs and came back with rabbits and hares and the women started to prepare a welcome meal. A few cockerels were killed and the tantalising smell of a large pot of *jogray* spread over the camp.

I went to see Gran and all she said was, 'Come and see me in the morning. Enjoy your welcome.' I tried to get her to say what was on her mind but her lips were as tight as a clam's shell. I did appreciate the warm homecoming and I really did try to show enjoyment but, oh God, I missed my little Sylvy, especially at a time like this and I wandered off by myself and shed a few more tears.

When I went back to the party, Gran was waiting for me. She instinctively knew what I had been doing. She took me by the hands and said quietly, 'George, I've told you before, it takes time, it will get easier. Young Sylvy will leave your head and you will carry her for always in your heart.' She released my hands and walked off back to her wagon, saying over her shoulder, 'We'll talk tomorrow.'

The drinking and feasting went on into the early hours; everybody was kind to me, but all I wanted to do was hide away and be by myself. The next morning I helped Dad with the horses and he chatted on as if nothing had happened. Whether or not he sensed a change in me and the fact that I had no intention of staying, he didn't show it and I told him nothing of my plans for the future. I would let him know after I had spoken to Gran.

Although it was gone midday, she was still lying abed and as I went into her wagon she said that her old bones were telling her to stay where she was. She held out her hand, which I took gently in mine. She looked at me straight in the eyes for several minutes before saying, 'I hope you settle in your new life. There will be a lot of difficulties but you'll be all right. Things will never be the same again and you won't be coming back to us. Many will disown you and it will hurt but you'll always be loved by your Dad – though he won't understand why you have to do these things. And you'll always be loved by me. I want you to promise me you'll come back and see me whenever you can and I won't rest in my grave if you don't come to my funeral. I'll tell them all they'll be cursed if they try to stop you.' I went to speak but she held up her hand to silence me. 'Say nothing, my boy. Gran sees all. Go and talk to your Dad and forgive him if he gets angry. He'll be worried about you going into the world of the *gorgio*.' She wiped away a few tears with her gnarled old hand, pulled the bed clothes over her head and in a muffled voice said, 'Good luck and take care of yourself.'

I found Dad in one of the workshops and told him about my friendship with the policeman and how he had told me about the Royal Air Force – how much he enjoyed it. I explained that I'd thought long and hard before making a decision to join the RAF but that I would be going in a few weeks' time. He was very disappointed in me and things got very heated, especially when he uncharitably said, 'I lost my first wife but I didn't run away.'

To which I retorted, 'You couldn't, you'd got *chavvies* (children) and I'm not running away. I need to get away and start again.'

The conversation went backwards and forwards and the comments got more vitriolic. He was upset but I was expecting more support and perhaps a little understanding from him and it took several days for us both to calm down. I kept away from him and passed the time doing repairs to an old wagon until, a few evenings after our bust-up, he poked his head into my wagon and said, 'I'm taking the dogs for a walk, will you come with me?' I was pleased that he had made the first approach because, given the mood I was in, I could have 'cut my nose off to spite my face'. He continued, 'We'll call at the Live (the Live and Let Live, a local pub) and have a few pints and a *pukker* (chat).' I agreed.

As we were about to leave the camp one of Dad's brothers, my Uncle John, who kept himself to himself and rarely spoke to anyone, much to our surprise asked if he could come with us. This was very unusual. Dad felt obliged to tell him we were going to call at the pub – this would normally put him off due to his acute meanness. It was said of him, 'He'd skin a gnat for the tallow!' But he still wanted to come so off we went, the three of us and a couple of lurchers. John was different from his brothers: he was tall and slim whereas the others were short and thickset. There had been many rumours about his origins but this was a subject best left alone!

We walked probably five to six miles and called into the pub. The dogs lay under the table and Dad fetched three pints of cider which were steadily drunk. I stood up and asked Dad and Uncle John if they wanted another and each nodded 'yes' so three more pints were brought to the table. Conversation got a bit easier as the booze loosened John's tongue – he was generally quite difficult to talk to. We sipped our drinks and chatted and slowly the glasses emptied. John looked at the three empty glasses, stood up and asked, 'You going to have another, Tom? You going to have another George?' to which we both said 'yes'. John said, 'I'll wait for you outside then,' turned on his heels and walked out. Dad and I looked at each other in amusement. Dad said, 'The tight-fisted bugger, he's too mean to buy us a pint,' and we laughed until the tears rolled down our cheeks. We stayed and had two more drinks; by the time we went outside John had gone, making his own way back to the camp. John's meanness had lightened the tension between me and Dad and on the way home we had a long talk. Dad ended up saying he would support me in anything I did and that there would be a place for me by his side when I returned from the RAF.

Some of my relatives were appalled to hear I was going into the world of the non-Gypsy; others were fascinated and wanted to know how I thought I would cope. My Uncle George taught me lots of basic drill and rifle drill. He also schooled me in how to 'bull' my boots and in fieldcraft and survival techniques. He really enjoyed having me marching up and down, shouting out his orders and reliving the past. George had served in the army from 1914 to 1919, and had taken part in many of the major battles of World War One, but his luck ran out in early 1918 when he was on the edge of a shell explosion, received multiple shrapnel wounds and was shipped back to England. On recovering, he was posted to a training camp as a drill corporal and when he started to drill me it didn't take long to get his old techniques back. Both of us took it all very seriously and it was indeed to stand me in good stead. When I asked him why he had volunteered for the army, he gave no patriotic 'King and Country' reason. He said he had been fifteen and out with a pony and small cart doing some *totting* (scrap-metal dealing) when he was confronted by three men who had obviously been drinking. They hurled abuse at him and tried to get the pony out of the shafts. Uncle George told me he picked up a piece of metal and laid one of the men out with a split head. As the other two rushed at him, he took a small sharp knife from his pocket and sliced off part of one their ears – the man let out a loud scream and ran round in circles. George leapt onto the pony and galloped back to where the family were camping. He quickly explained to his Dad what had happened, shoved a few belongings into a bag and no one saw him again for over two years. He had seen a recruiting parade in the local town, lied about his age and was accepted into the army with very few questions asked.

The most important thing Uncle George told me was that everything would be different from what I had been used to; I would have to adapt quickly to the *gorgio* world and try and put aside lifelong traditions and taboos. If I didn't do this I would be picked on and bullied. 'Remember,' he said, 'in the long run it's easier for you to fall in with the majority than for the majority to change their ways to yours. It'll be hard but if you want to be accepted and succeed, you've got to do it.' I never forgot those words.

I continued to work with the horses until my papers came with a one-way rail-travel warrant and directions to the RAF induction camp at Cardington near Bedford.

15

Change of Life

Dad dropped me off at the station, handed me my holdall and gave me a wad of money. He shook me by the hand, wished me good luck, turned the horse and trap round and went back up the street without a wave or a backward glance. Dad hardly ever showed any sentiment. There were only a few other people on the platform, one lot stood out from the others. This was a middle-aged couple with a young man who looked as if he was their son – they were all crying. I looked away and moved further down the platform. The train drew in, I found an empty compartment and prepared to settle down when the wet-eyed young man came in and sat down just as the train was pulling out. I felt embarrassed when he began to sob, so I asked him what the matter was and he explained he had never been away from home before, not even for one night. Now he had been called up to do his national service in the RAF and was also on his way to RAF Cardington. He couldn't believe it when I told him I'd lived by myself for nigh on two years. I told him a little bit about my life, the way we Travellers lived and, to show him he wasn't the only one with problems, I also mentioned Sylvy. He stopped crying and said how sorry he was and in the same breath asked if he could be with me when we got to the camp. When I found out his name was Gordon Pratt, I remained tight-lipped and passed not a comment!

At Bedford station we boarded a Royal Air Force bus and, along with other new recruits, we were driven to the reception camp. On arrival we were lined up in a column of threes in height order, after which we were given a lecture by a flight sergeant which was only memorable for being unmemorable. We were shown to our billets. I managed to get a bed by the door where it was draughty – no one else wanted it. Gordon Pratt got the bed next to mine. Lined up in threes again, we were marched to the cookhouse where we were introduced to military food. Revolting! The meal was stone cold and consisted of lumpy mashed potato, processed-pea skins – where the actual peas were, I don't know – and watery, overcooked smoked haddock, followed by stodgy sago pudding with a dollop of damson jam consisting mainly of stones. And it didn't get any better for the short while I was there. As far as I was concerned, most of the food went straight into the bin – a receptacle I was to see a lot of.

The following morning we were lined up, taken to the clothing stores and kitted out in the most monotonous way: 'Boots, two number for the use of; beret, one number for the use of; peaked cap, one number for the use of' and so it went on. What a soul-destroying job. Back at the hut, we changed into our working blues and yet again lined up in threes whilst we were inspected by a short, fat, pompous sergeant who every now and again poked a recruit with his stick and passed some comment which was meant obviously to amuse himself. As he stood in front of me my beret, which, although I'd asked for a size 6 ⅞ths, was a size 10 (or so it seemed), slipped slowly down my forehead and covered my eyes and nose, causing a great deal of amusement to everyone except the sergeant who roared, 'You 'orrible little airman. If you 'ad wanted to be a comedian you should 'ave gone on the bleeding stage.'

I pushed my hat up just as he poked me with his stick and said, 'I appear to have a turd on the end of my stick,' to which I stupidly said, 'I know, I'm looking at it'. The sergeant's eyes bulged, his face turned scarlet and the veins on his neck enlarged and stuck right out. He ordered the laughter to stop immediately – which it did. He called to a corporal to take over and I was taken to the guardhouse where I was locked in a cell. I couldn't believe it: I'd been in the RAF for less than two days and here I was banged up in a cell. The feeling of claustrophobia was devastating. I hated closed-in spaces. I was on the verge of panic and sweating profusely when the eyehole was lifted and someone looked in. The door was unlocked and a white-cap (RAFP) sergeant came in. 'What have you been up to lad?' he asked so I told him. He burst out laughing and surprisingly was sympathetic towards me. I don't really know why, but I told him about my background and, instead of the usual derogatory and prejudiced remarks, he was interested and called the two duty corporals to listen as well. The police sergeant explained I would be up in front of the squadron leader in the morning and said that he would probably give me a rollocking and let it go at that.

It wasn't quite that simple. I did have a dressing down by the squadron leader but was put on evening cookhouse duties. Which meant that whilst the other new recruits were having a pint in the NAAFI I was washing up hundreds of dirty crocks. No more than I deserved for being the smart-arse! I kept quiet for the rest of the week.

Several of us, including Gordon Pratt, were posted to the training camp at Padgate near Warrington in Lancashire. What a depressing place Padgate was. Thick fog, mizzling rain, mud everywhere and nearly everyone had a cough. Everything was done at the double and everybody was constantly shouted at. We were allocated to huts and I was pleased 'our Gordon' was in a different hut, but even this caused embarrassment. On hearing he wasn't to be with me, he asked the sergeant if he could swap over as he wanted to be with his friend. 'No you bleeding well can't,' bawled the sergeant. 'You'll go where you've been put. What are you, a pair of bleeding jessies? If we find you doing things like that you'll spend the rest of your life in the glasshouse!'

I remembered Uncle George's words about having to accept 'unacceptable' standards as the *gorgios'* life was different to ours. The thing I missed most was privacy. Early one morning a corporal came in, made all of us stand to attention by our beds and told us the doctor would be there in a few minutes time to do a 'short arm' inspection to check whether any of us had any obvious sexual transmitted diseases. Forty men all standing there as naked as the day they were born. Some were giggling like schoolkids, others were acutely embarrassed, whilst others – mainly those with the large appendages – were very proud of themselves. The doctor went slowly down one side of the hut and back up the other, stopping at each airman, lifting up his willy and testicles with a cane stick and peering at them closely. He made many well-worn comments which generated much nervous laughter. To some unfortunates he suggested they would be better off in the Women's Royal Air Force, to others he said, 'Do you realise it's against the law to have an offensive weapon?' He paused in front of one small skinny lad, raised his voice so everyone could hear how funny he was, and said, 'Good God! Have you stolen something from the snake house or was it the way your mother lifted you in and out of the bath?' He paused for the laughter and then continued, 'Corporal, make a note this man is to be issued with a pair of boxing gloves and he is to wear them in bed every night.' More laughter. You could see the poor lad just wanted to curl up and die but he wasn't as upset as the young man standing next to him. The doctor looked aghast as he viewed the airman's bright red parts: 'What in hell's name have you been up to? Where have you been putting it? You don't keep chickens, do you?' These remarks caused further laughter and the young man's face grew as red as his private parts. 'After I've finished here, follow me over to sick quarters,' continued the medical man. A few days later the unfortunate airman returned, completely back to normal. The redness was known as a *dhobi* (washing) rash, which happens if underclothes are not thoroughly rinsed during washing – but the medics had had to make sure he didn't have anything catching.

My introduction to Drill Corporal Barber, a big ginger-haired Scotsman (known as Ali behind his back) was not a good one and we got off to a very bad start. He had a voice which would eclipse any town crier's and used it to full effect whenever the opportunity arose. He was also a bully. The fact that I was from a travelling family had not been used in a derogatory way so far. To my surprise, most of my new colleagues were interested and asked a lot of positive questions. This ended when Barber entered the hut early one morning. Everyone stood to attention by their beds. He stared at everyone in turn, then bellowed, 'Which one of you is the Gyppo?' Before I could answer, he continued, with a smile on his face. 'We've never had a Gyppo before, this could be quite interesting. Come on, don't be shy. Which one of you is it?'

I stepped forward and said, 'I'm from a travelling family, if that's what you mean.' He swaggered down the hut, stood in front of me with his face close to mine and bawled, 'Haven't you forgotten something, Airman?' When I didn't answer he shouted, 'Corporal! I'm from a travelling family, Corporal! Do I make myself clear?'

'Yes Corporal.'

'So you're the Gyppo, are you?'

'No,' I replied, 'I'm not a Gyppo. I have Gypsy blood in my veins and I'm from a travelling family but I am not a Gyppo. To call someone a Gyppo is an insult, Corporal.'

'As if I care. If I say you're a Gyppo, you're a Gyppo, is that clear?'

'No, I will not be called a Gyppo.' And before he could say anything I went on, 'You wouldn't like it if I called you "Ginger balls".' At which point he exploded.

'You, Airman, are on a two-five-two (charge) for gross insubordination.' He demanded my twelve-fifty (identification), made notes and told me to report to the administration block at 08.30 hours. Then he stomped out.

The lads gathered round me in the hut and said they would all support me and would be witnesses to what had taken place. At 08.30 hours I was marched into a flight lieutenant's office and the charge was read out. Barber gave his version of events, which was untrue. He stated that, during a normal conversation, I had without cause rudely referred to him as 'Ginger balls' (I'm sure I saw the officer's mouth twitch). I was asked if I had anything to say and I told the officer the true version, and I finished up by saying that there were over twenty witnesses standing outside who would corroborate my story. I also added that I would like to pursue a redress of grievance against the corporal. I was asked to stand outside whilst the officer and the corporal spoke together. When I went back in Barber was very red in the face and looked extremely crestfallen. The flight lieutenant said, 'Charge dismissed' and looked across at the corporal, who said, 'I wish to apologise for referring to you as a Gyppo. I was not aware it was a derogatory remark.' The officer asked if I accepted the apology and I said, 'Yes, Sir'. Barber was dismissed and when he had gone I was asked whether or not I wished to carry on with the redress of grievance. The flight lieutenant explained that Barber had just been stupid but that I was entitled to go on with the 'redress', although it would most certainly harm his career if I did so. I was under no obligation to withdraw my application, but as the corporal had apologised would I consider it? I saw an opportunity to keep Barber off my back so I agreed to withdraw. The corporal still shouted and swaggered but he didn't pick on me again.

I really threw myself into the routine and I enjoyed the challenge of learning something new. I did nothing to antagonise Ali Barber and he grudgingly said to me once that I was doing well. Praise indeed! I took pride in my appearance and everything was bulled, pressed or polished so my turnout was always to a high standard. I loved being on the firing range and was a first-class shot with the .22 rifle and the .303. I also won the inter-camp shooting contest – which pleased Ali.

I took part in the boxing competition and to my everlasting shame I lost in the first fight – I couldn't believe it. The only consolation was that the boxer who beat me went on to be the overall winner. I kept thinking Dad would be ashamed of me – I fought like a fairy with a powder puff, I had no power in my punches and my timing was abysmal. After the three rounds I'd finished up with two black eyes and a swollen nose. Towards the end of my basic training, I had a chance to make amends and redeem my self-respect in another contest. This time I got as far as the semi-finals, losing on points to the same contestant as before, only this time it was a close split decision and his was a Pyrrhic victory as he was in a more battered state than me.

The food was abysmal. I understood that the cooks went to catering school for several weeks and learned how to ruin good food. All our cooks must have passed with flying colours! I would eat the breakfast, normally consisting of overcooked bacon, hard fried eggs, undercooked sausages and beans. You also had a choice of porridge – some days you could have it sliced, other days you asked for so many lumps! I filled up on bread, gave lunch a miss and then went to see what was for evening meal. If it looked reasonable I would try it. I love *jogray* and one night there was mutton stew on the menu. I got my helping, but when I looked at my plate it was full of big lumps of fat, gristle and bones, absolutely inedible. So it was off to the NAAFI to fill up on battered jam sandwiches. Lovely!

I really liked working out in the gym and looked forward to the assault course - over the high wall, through the submerged tunnel, up the nets, over the rope bridge, swinging from the bridge platform and down another set of nets, over the logs above deep mud and water, leap from stepping stone to stepping stone through a sea of mud, and finally underneath a large tarpaulin – by which time you were well and truly tatered – only to be confronted by the two final obstacles – up a twenty-foot rope onto a platform, then swing to a net, climb down and run to the finish (and collapse!).

I loved the competition, platoon against platoon – I never came first but was generally in the first ten out of a hundred-plus.

We were taught survival techniques and had been told we would have a chance to put them into practice towards the end of our basic training. Some of the recruits weren't looking forward to this – I was and couldn't wait to do it. There were another two weeks to wait and before it took place we were due a long weekend's leave after six weeks at Padgate. I hadn't seen much of Gordon Pratt as he was in a different platoon from me, but we met again on Warrington station and agreed to travel back together – in just six weeks he had changed and was becoming more mature now he was away from his parents.

I arrived home to a subdued greeting. Not that they weren't pleased to see me, they were. Dad explained that a prayer had been answered: Milletti (Sylvy's mom) was seriously ill and had been praying for me to come home so she could see me again. I changed out of my uniform and went across to Sam and Milletti's wagon. I met Sam outside – he looked ill with worry himself. He cautioned me to be prepared for a shock when I saw his wife and when I did see her I was still shocked in spite of the warning. She had lost so much weight she'd almost wasted away altogether. She was skeletal and her eyes had sunk back into her head with big dark rings round them. She smiled when she saw me, showing her lovely white teeth that looked too big for her mouth, raised her bony arm and held my hand in her clawlike hand. When she spoke it was difficult to hear her now-rasping voice but I managed to make out that she was so pleased to see me and she could now join little Sylvy and tell her how I looked.

It took all my willpower not to burst out crying – this was the woman who had taken me when I was but a few hours old, nurtured me with her body and raised me as if I was her own. She held tightly to my hand until she lapsed into an uneasy sleep. I gently let go of her and went outside where I could no longer control my emotion. I went to see Gran and she told me, 'Before you go back, make sure you see Milletti because you won't see her again, but we will see you at her funeral.' I never questioned her because Gran always seemed to know. I stayed in her wagon, telling her about my time with the *gorgios* and how I found it hard to adjust. She listened and all she said was, 'It was your choice. You'll be all right though.' She paused then continued, 'Listen to your old Gran, my boy. You've already had your heart broken once, so beware *gorgio raklies* (non-Gypsy girls), find a *Romany chi* (lass) and you'll be *boktalo* (happy).' She changed the subject and wouldn't say any more; I left her wagon as she closed her eyes and nodded off.

I spent a lot of time with Milletti simply holding her hand and talking to her; occasionally she would open her eyes and smile and then drift off again. Before I returned to Padgate I called to see her again and she was quite lucid. I explained I'd be back in about three weeks' time and I would see her then, to which she replied, 'If God wishes.' I kissed her clammy brow and left, knowing I wouldn't see her alive again.

The return journey to the training camp was torturous. Gordon Pratt talked incessantly about what he'd done during his seventy-two hour pass, what his mom had said, what his dad had said and what their neighbours had said: how smart he was in his uniform. I could have screamed – all I could think about was Aunty Milletti. I didn't say anything as I didn't want to spoil his good mood but, oh, what a blessing when we got to the camp and he went to his own hut.

Much to my disappointment, the survival exercise had been cancelled, all we were going to do was be dropped off at an unknown destination and make our way back. As we were told, 'initiative is the key'. It was mid-December, bitter cold but dry. We were dressed in our fatigues (under which I had two vests, two shirts, a short-sleeved pullover, jersey and a scarf), belt, boots, gaiters, gloves and waterproof capes. We all had a full water bottle and a knapsack containing sandwiches (with some dubious filling), two bars of chocolate and a bar of Kendal mint cake. We set off in the dark. We had travelled for well over two hours when the lorry pulled over and stopped and we all got out. The driver shouted 'Good luck' and drove off. The night was clear and the sky was full of stars; the wind went straight through your clothes despite all the layers. Our eyes adjusted quickly and we could soon make out the lie of the land – there wasn't a light to be seen, which meant no farms, no houses.

Someone suggested we head back in the direction the lorry had brought us.

'How do you know we weren't going round in circles? You could be going completely the wrong way,' I said.

'Well, what are you going to do then, smart-arse?' retorted the airman who'd mooted the suggestion.

'I'm going to find somewhere to shelter and start off at first light. If you set off now you could make things worse,' I countered.

'You'll freeze to death if you stay out here, you bloody fool. It's best to keep moving. Who's going to follow me?' he shouted. Everybody except one airman, a lad called Peter Griffin (who soon became a friend for life), headed off with the self-appointed leader. I said to Peter that the first thing we must do was get out of the wind. I looked around and I could see clumps of gorse and a lot of bracken. We pushed our way into the middle of a clump of gorse bushes where there was a hollow about six feet wide and long and about three foot deep. Lying in the hollow and protected by the gorse bushes, we were sheltered from the wind. We ate a couple of sandwiches, still not being able to work out what the filling was, had a drink of water, then we left the protection of the bushes and gathered armfuls of bracken. Half of the dead ferns we placed in the bottom of the depression then we laid one of our waterproof capes over the top of them on which Peter lay. I put the other cape over him, then placed the remainder of the bracken on top. Finally I crawled in under the cape. Lying next to each other, with our combined body heat and the insulation from the covering, we were soon quite warm. Peter started to chuckle and said, 'I wish you were a wench!' I told him to sod off and we soon went to sleep.

We were woken by the sound of voices. I cautiously raised myself up and peered through the bracken. To my horror, a woman had pushed her way through the gorse bushes, lifted her skirt and was just about to lower her pants when Peter coughed. The woman stood open-mouthed as two bracken-clad apparitions appeared out of the ground. She let out an almighty scream and ran out of the gorse bushes still screaming. In seconds six men appeared, some with their fists raised, others brandishing objects with which to attack us. We quickly explained who we were and what we were doing and showed them our RAF identification badges. Once they were confident we were who we said we were, they visibly relaxed. It turned out they were a local cycling club out on an early morning ride. They had stopped for a breather and one of the women had popped into the bushes to relieve herself. She was embarrassed and so were Pete and me, but we all had a good laugh.

We found out from the cyclists that we were in the Peak District, near the Blue John Cavern, and by looking at the bike club maps we worked out the route to take us to Buxton. I knew my way around that area as several of my relations camped near there quite regularly and our field given to us by the Judge wasn't far away either. Being young and fit, we ran two miles, walked a short distance and then ran two more miles. In this way we covered the ground at a good speed. When we got to Buxton we treated ourselves to a breakfast in a 'Smokey Joe's' and prepared to thumb a lift to Macclesfield or further, maybe to Knutsford.

As we left the cafe we saw an attractive middle-aged woman loaded down with bags walking down the street. We asked her if we could help her carry them, she flashed us a lovely smile and with a strong southern American accent accepted our offer, explaining she was on her way to the car park to meet her husband. We took the bags from her and went to where the car was parked. It was a brand new Pontiac, 'flown over from the States for us a few weeks ago,' she said.

Suddenly we heard a deep, growling voice say, 'Hi Hon, these two harassing you?' We turned and saw that the growl had come from a giant, about six foot six and built like an outside toilet, sporting a close-cropped crewcut and puffing on a huge cigar.

'Why no, Chucky, these boys have been helping me with my bags. Ain't that just sweet?'

'Chucky' thanked us, then offered us payment which we politely refused. He introduced himself as Master Sergeant

Chuck Elwes of the USAF and the woman was his wife Betty-May. They had taken a week's furlough, he explained, and had been exploring the Peak District. Now they were heading back to the US Air Force camp at Burtonwood. We told him who we were and what we were doing, and at the mention of us making our way to Padgate he whistled and said, 'Boys, this is your lucky day. Burtonwood is only a few miles from your camp. I'll take you right up to the gates.'

Lady Luck was with us that day. Pete and me got into the back seat of the car and sank down in sheer luxury. It was like sitting in a comfy armchair. The car had every luxury, great heater, radio, record player, big leather seats, no surface noise and the ride was so smooth that the two of us went to sleep mid-conversation and didn't wake up until we were nearly at Padgate. The two Americans only laughed when we tried to apologise. Betty-May said, 'No need to be sorry, boys, you must have been plum-tuckered.'

True to his word, Chuck dropped us off outside the gates, gave us his card and invited us to call and see them anytime. We weren't first back – five others had got back before us, but we scored valuable points for our platoon and we came second overall. Some didn't get back for several days and were accused of deliberately abusing the situation. Two lads never came back at all: we didn't get to know the end of that story as we left Padgate two weeks later.

Most of the intake had been allocated the trade they'd requested, some were disappointed. When it came to me, there appeared to be a problem. I'd changed my mind about the RAFP as I was having doubts about becoming a policeman and had put that as my second choice. My first preference was now to be an armourer – I loved anything to do with weapons. I was informed that, due to the long training period, I would have to sign on for five years to become an armourer. I wasn't prepared to do this so I was told they were going 'to set a thief to catch a thief' and they put me in the Royal Air Force Police. I ignored the obvious slur that assumed all Gypsies are thieves.

After the eight weeks' basic training we had the passing-out parade which was a pomp-and-splendour occasion attended by several senior RAF officers; many parents had come to see the spectacle as well. At the end we were issued with our passes and rail warrants to the trade training camp, said our farewells, and headed home for a few days' leave before, in my case, reporting to the RAFP training school at Netheravon in Wiltshire.

Dad was at the station to meet me. He greeted me with a brief handshake and told me Milletti had died and that the funeral was the next day. Not the homecoming I had hoped for but not unexpected. Greetings were subdued and I spent the night keeping vigil over Milletti until it was time for the burial. There were over three hundred people from all over the country at the funeral with lorry-loads of wreaths of all shapes and designs. Sam was well-pleased with the way everything went and, although it was a sad occasion, he enjoyed all the attention he got.

No one wanted to miss the ceremony so, with Sam's blessing and understanding, I stayed in the camp and looked after Gran who couldn't get there as she was suffering from a bout of bronchitis. We talked about Aunty Milletti but most of all we chatted about little Sylvy – it still hurt but at least I could talk about her without breaking down now. I reckon Gran always spoke about Sylvy when I was with her to get me to talk and gradually lessen the pain.

The wake was well attended, there was no unseemly behaviour, all went quietly and most set off back home early next morning, leaving poor old Sam to start preparing for life on his own. During the rest of my leave I spent a lot of time walking and talking about both mother and daughter with Uncle Sam. On one occasion we drowned our sorrows by calling in the pub as soon as it opened in the morning and not leaving until they chucked us out at closing time. We must have cut a comical picture because Dad told me everyone came out from their wagons or stopped what they were doing to watch us. Arms wrapped round each other, each trying to hold the other up, only to get our feet in a robble and lie down on the lane, laughing fit to bust.

I wasn't laughing the next morning, having slept right through the afternoon and the night. I felt as if my head was inside a striking cathedral bell – it even hurt to move my eyes. I went back to bed and stayed there until the following morning when I felt a lot better. Poor Sam was still feeling poorly and even resorted to one of Gran's cures, a foul-tasting emetic. A few hours later, after clearing out his system, he felt a lot better and vowed he would never get drunk again. In fact he said, 'I'd rather never touch another drop of *levinar* (ale) ever again if it meant I hadn't got to take old Louie's *drab* (medicine)!'

Before leaving for Netheravon the next day I called to see Gran again. She was crystal-gazing and as I went in she looked up with a troubled look on her face.

'What can you see Gran?' I asked her.

'I see a lot of feet and running between them is a *bitti hatchi-witchu* (little hedgehog). The feet are trying to stamp on or kick the little animal – now the feet are running away as the *hatchi-witchu* is getting bigger and bigger and bigger and trying to bite them. It's fading, now it's gone.'

'What's it mean, Gran?'

Before answering, she carefully covered her crystal ball and put it back on the shelf. Then she looked directly into my eyes and said, 'You're going to be unhappy for a while. The *bitti hatchi-witchu* is you, the feet belong to *gorgios* who don't like you, but you'll come out on top. Don't give up. Fight!' She wouldn't say any more.

A few hours later I was on the train to Netheravon.

16

Police Training –
Royal Air Force Police

As soon as I went through the gates of Netheravon camp I experienced a feeling of foreboding and felt uncomfortable – was it because of Gran's dire warning? Would I have had these feelings if Gran had said nothing? Perhaps. Or was there a genuine feeling of unease? Maybe. Whatever, I decided to throw myself fully into the course, to keep myself to myself as much as I could and try not to get distracted. But as I was to find out, sixteen weeks was a long time.

I enjoyed all aspects of the course. I'd already been driving for many years but had never passed the official test: by the end of the course I could drive legally, having passed my test in Salisbury. I enjoyed the weaponry training and learning self-defence, as well as all the time spent in the gym. A lot of the time was spent in the classroom learning about criminal law, interview techniques, how to conduct an investigation, the use of the baton and handcuffs, how to make an arrest and methods of restraint.

On our first day, after the instructor had introduced himself, we all had to stand up one by one and give details of our background. When it came to my turn, I gave vague details saying that I had been born in the Black Country, that we were horse-breeders and dealers and left it at that. But the instructor had other ideas and asked me to say where I was educated and where I lived. When I said I hadn't been to school, that we'd had teachers come to us, a strong Welsh voice shouted out, 'Christ, like the bloody Queen!' which created a deal of laughter. The sergeant then asked, 'Where did you live, then, tell us about that.' I wasn't going to lie, so I told them the truth. The same Welsh voice from the back of the room piped up again, saying, 'I didn't think any bloody Diddies (Diddekois) could read or write.' The instructor told him to keep quiet.

I turned and saw that the Welshman was well-made with broad shoulders, a scowling face and narrow eyes. I took an instant dislike to him, not only because of his snide remarks, and I realised that if I let him get the better of me now it would become much worse. I said in Romanes, *'Tute si o bora mowied dinnelo'* ('You're a big-mouthed fool'). He bridled and demanded to know what I'd said. I knew I'd needled him. I smiled and merely said, 'That's the advantage I've got, I can say anything I like and you won't know what I'm saying.' The sergeant called us to order and said we were to report to him after the lesson.

At the end of the instruction period we were taken into a small office where the sergeant said, 'You two boys have got off to a bad start. I want you to shake hands and start again. If you refuse, you'll be kicked off the course and you'll spend the rest of your service as an admin orderly, picking up litter, cleaning toilets and running errands. Is that clear?'

We both replied, 'Yes, sergeant.'

I found out later that the Welshman's name was Ingram and he was in for twelve years. He thrust out his hand but his eyes showed it wasn't a genuine gesture. I took his hand, quickly, making sure his fingers were all together and he couldn't exert any pressure on mine whilst I squeezed his hand as hard as I could. I saw him wince and then let go. As we went out of the room the instructor said, 'I'll be keeping an eye on you two.' We both knew this wouldn't be the end of the enmity between us. At every opportunity when there were no staff about, Ingram would pass some sort of derogatory comment about Travellers. At one tea break he was his usual obnoxious self so I went to the front of the classroom whilst the instructor was out of the room, held up my hand and asked the class to be quiet for a few moments. I then said, 'You all know about my background and the way Ingram keeps making snide references to it. Well, what you probably don't know and Ingram doesn't want you to know is that one of the most predominant tribes of Romanies in Wales is the Ingrams.'

Ingram flushed in anger and shouted, 'I'm not related to any bloody Gyppos...' At this point he was shouted down by a lot of the others who asked me to go on, so I did.

'Look at him – dark, swarthy, thickset, all the traits of the Ingram Romanies.' The majority of the lads were with me; the only ones who weren't were his clique of 'weak-chins' who hung around him and were part of his card school. He was moving towards me as the instructor walked in, so Ingram merely whispered that he would 'get me'.

The sergeant instructing us was the same one who had made us shake hands and he asked us if we were getting on all right? I couldn't resist telling him about the Ingrams and the fact that my adversary could also be of Traveller blood.

'Well, well, Ingram, that's interesting. So all the time you've been ridiculing Locke – the staff are well aware of it, by the way – it was to take the attention off yourself.'

Ingram, flushed with anger, started to protest but was told
to shut up. At the end of the lesson we were again taken into
an office where we were told that all the staff knew about the
bad blood between us and were also aware of Ingram's stupid
comments. We were ordered to 'cut it out' – if we didn't it
could end in disaster for one or both of us.

As we walked away, and out of earshot of the sergeant,
Ingram threatened, 'You'll pay for this, you bastard, I'll make
sure you regret it. You'll be sorry you were born.'

I smiled at him and riled him even further by saying,
'Don't you think it would be better if we fellow Travellers
stuck together?' I saw his fists clench and as I walked away
I said, '*Tute si o bul hev*. I'll translate it as you don't know the
language of your ancestors. It means, "You're an arsehole".'
He was so angry I thought he was going to cry; he couldn't
do anything there and then as a lot of people were milling
about.

A short while afterwards things were brought to a head.
I'd been for a drink in the NAAFI with a couple of the lads.
Surprisingly, Ingram and his cronies weren't there. We went
back to the hut to find the Welshman and his creeps and
others I didn't know playing cards. I was tired and decided
to have an early night. The nearer I got to my bed the
stronger I could smell something and I realised most of those
playing cards were watching. Then I noticed a lump in the
middle of the bed and, on pulling back the clothes, I saw a
dead squashed hedgehog full of maggots with a note saying,
'Perhaps you would like this for breakfast.' I said not a word.
I picked up the note and put it in my pocket, removed the
top blankets and wrapped the smelly hedgehog in the top and
bottom sheet to try and stop the smell getting out and locked
it in my wardrobe. I hadn't been particularly close to anyone

in the hut but this action appalled everyone who wasn't one of Ingram's pals. No one would speak to them. When asked what I intended to do, I simply said, 'You'll see tomorrow.' I pulled my bed out and pushed it in front of my wardrobe so no one could break the lock and take the evidence during the night.

First thing in the morning I went over to the admin block and explained what had happened to a Warrant Officer. We went outside and I unwrapped the decidedly rank hedgehog. The WO was not amused. I filled in a report and left the next step to him. Midway through our first lecture, the same WO and two sergeants in full uniform and 'Mars bars' (RAF Police armbands) came into the room. The lesson was suspended whilst each airman was called out individually and interviewed in a separate office. The last one to be interrogated was Ingram. After an hour he came back looking very pale and worried. His circle of 'friends' were then re-interrogated, after which the policemen left. I was ordered to see the WO, who told me that they would find the culprit, they had a strong suspect and it was only a matter of time before one of his cronies cracked.

Ingram and his clique were transferred to another hut and forbidden to leave the camp. The rest of the lads became friendly and I spent that evening revising for the next exam with an airman called James Lancaster − known to everyone as Burt. Later on we went to the NAAFI, had a few pints of beer, returned to the hut and turned in. About five o'clock in the morning the door was flung open by two corporals who ordered me to get dressed and accompany them. I was taken to the guardhouse and told to wait. After half an hour or so the same WO and a flight lieutenant took me into an office and asked me where I'd been last evening. I was told to write down every minute detail of my whereabouts during the hours from seven o'clock to ten thirty, who I was with, who I saw, what I was doing. They wouldn't answer any questions; they both closely inspected my hands and after removing my shoes they inspected them as well. When all this had been completed I was escorted back to the hut where my locker and wardrobe were searched and my belt and boots examined. The mattress was taken off my bed and searched. I had no idea what was going on so I asked the WO again what it was all about. He looked at me and said, 'I hope to Christ it wasn't you and you had nothing to do with it, because if it was, you'll be more or less sent to Hell.'

'What? What am I under suspicion of, Sir?' I cried in alarm. 'What is it?'

'If your statement checks out – and at the moment we're interviewing Lancaster – you've nothing to worry about and someone may have done you a favour. Your "friend" Ingram was found by the perimeter fence just about alive. He's had one hell of a beating and kicking by someone who knew what they were doing – it looks like a professional job. In twenty-five years doing this job I've never seen anything like it.'

James Lancaster's statement bore out what I had said so suspicion moved from me. After a while we heard through the grapevine that Ingram had got mixed up with a gambling syndicate prior to joining the RAF and owed a lot of money he couldn't pay. We never found out what finally happened to him. On request I withdrew my complaint about the hedgehog. With my main distraction gone, I concentrated fully on the course and passed out with reasonable marks in the final exam and a good assessment on my report.

We were given our postings and several of us decided to go to London for a couple of days and celebrate. A cockney lad said we could stay at his house and he would show us London. I don't think his Mom was too pleased initially when seven of us descended on her but she put a brave face on it. We went 'up West' and our London friend enjoyed taking us around salacious Soho, as it was in the Fifties. We'd never seen such things on show before and couldn't understand how they could get away with being so brazen and the police taking no action. Having said that, we enjoyed the experience. The following day we meant to see some sights but we called into an East End pub on the way and by the time we got into the West End we were well and truly *matto* (drunk). The evening rush hour had started at about four thirty and we stood watching a very harassed policeman in the middle of the road directing the traffic; he was getting more and more frustrated and bad-tempered. Then someone, I forget who, mooted an idea. We drew lots to see who would do it and I pulled the short straw. From a bombsite left over from the War we found a brick and a length of old cord. We secured the brick to one end of the cord, the other end was looped round my neck and I stupidly dodged through the traffic till I reached the by now very red-faced policeman.

'Excuse me, Officer, can you tell me the way to the Thames?' He didn't seem to appreciate the humour of the situation. He stopped all the traffic and, towering over me, he shouted, 'You bleeding idiot, you could have got yourself killed. Ain't I got enough to do without having to put up with you buggering about? I'm being relieved in ten minutes – if I see you still round here I'll put my boot up your backside so far you won't see any laceholes. Now bugger off before I lock you up.'

Somewhat chastened, I made my way back to where my mates were doubled up with laughter. The irate policeman was glowering and mouthing at us so we beat a hasty retreat before someone took over from him. We enjoyed our short time in the capital before going our separate ways home and then on to our postings.

The camp I was posted to was a small radar station in the heart of the Cheshire countryside. It was in two parts, the main camp and a few miles away the radar installations and a semi-sunk bunker. I found it friendly and welcoming, with a great atmosphere, and I settled in very quickly. A few miles away there was a lovely little market town with some great pubs. I'd only been at the camp a few days when I was invited to a demob party – these happened on a regular basis as there were a lot of two-year national servicemen who were sent to the camp in a continual stream and who therefore left at the same rate.

One evening we decided to see how many pubs we could get round by having a half pint in each. I was the first to drop out after we had visited eighteen pubs and I spent the night sleeping in a gateway to a field. When I woke up I was covered in a thick hoar frost and couldn't stop shivering. I managed to get back in time to go on duty, only to be sent to sick quarters as I obviously had a chill and was dithering and shaking. I didn't tell the duty officer or hospital staff how I'd caught the chill!

There was a small NAAFI which did one of my favourites – battered jam sandwiches! It was run by a manager and two elderly ladies – one was very eccentric and dressed in shabby tweeds and drove up from town in a beaten-up soft-top Austin 7. The other looked like a female version of Toad of Toad Hall, with thinning jet-black hair and a Cupid's-bow mouth drawn on in lipstick. They were a pantomime producer's dream!

One evening I was off duty and having a drink in the NAAFI before going to town. The Toad lady had just arrived to relieve the other one and I overheard their conversation, which was being held in loud whispers.

'My dear,' said Mrs Toad, 'You'll never guess what happened to me on my way home last night after finishing here?' Before the tweedy woman could answer, she continued, 'I was cycling down the lane when I saw that airman Taylor walking back to camp and he was staggering all over the road. I foolishly stopped to ask him if he was all right. He never answered. He grabbed hold of me, dragged me into the field and "had his way with me" and then he left me lying there.'

'Oh you poor dear, what a brute,' her friend commented, but the storyteller wasn't listening, she simply carried on with her tale. 'It's very embarrassing, everyone will get to know, because he threw my bloomers up a tree and they're still there now. I was so ashamed as I went past them this evening.'

'Are you going to report him to the police?' asked the concerned woman.

The victim of the attack paused before answering and then said, 'I don't think so – perhaps he'll do it again!'

The other woman tutted and said, 'I haven't had a man in me since nineteen forty-three, and that was a big black American. Afterwards I said to myself, "Mildred, what's just happened to you is enough to last you for the rest of your life", and it has been.'

I mentioned what I'd heard to the sergeant and all he said was, 'If she doesn't complain, there's nothing we can do about it. I expect she was grateful.' On the way to town, exactly as she had described, there hanging from the tree was a large pair of pink double-reinforced-gusset directoire knickers.

They were there for a long time, slowly deteriorating. Every time anyone from the camp went past them, if you were in uniform you saluted (even the officers joined in), if in civvies you nodded to them or raised your hat. Vehicle-drivers blew their horns.

Most of the lads looked forward to the camp dances. Notices would be posted in the nearby town and on the evening itself car- and coachloads of young (and not so young) 'ladies' would arrive at the camp – oh, and a few men as well. Inevitably, the local men didn't like the girls getting too friendly with the lads from the camp and it usually ended up in a fight. If I wasn't on duty the night of the dance, I would volunteer for extra duty so that I could legally get involved in the melée on the pretext of trying to stop it or make an arrest. Unfortunately, the dances were stopped indefinitely after no one would own up to tying a used contraceptive on the door handle of the CO's office.

I was on duty with a Scottish corporal named McKay, Ginge to his friends, when we received a phonecall saying Taylor – the same one who had been involved with the Toad woman – was on his way back to camp and he was fighting drunk, having knocked out a couple of men in the pub. He was about five foot eleven inches and weighed around sixteen stone and was extraordinarily strong. Whenever he could, he worked out in the gym. Now in his thirties, he had been in the RAF for years and was still an AC1 (Aircraftsman First Class). He was an admin orderly, a euphemism for an odd-job man and general dogsbody. When he was sober he was okay but when drunk he was vicious and extremely violent. We – Ginge and me – decided discretion was the best part of valour and we agreed to keep watch but open the gates so he could walk straight in and go to his hut. Just as we were sitting debating this, the new Provost Sergeant, Mellor arrived. He was a pompous self-opinionated sort of man, fond of recounting many exaggerated acts of bravery. Corporal McKay said, 'We're glad you're here, Sarge. Taylor's on his way up from town and it'll take the three of us to handle him if he kicks off. None of us could manage him on our own, not even you, Sarge.' Not only was the hook and bait taken but also the line and sinker. Sergeant Mellor puffed out his chest and said, 'Are you suggesting I couldn't make an arrest on my own? I'll show you pair of "lily-livered" sods how to overcome your man Taylor.' He went outside towards the gate, saying, 'I don't need your help – stay in here.'

Just then Taylor started kicking the gates and shouting. The Sergeant told the drunken airman to shut up, to which he replied, 'Go away!' (in so many words). Mellor opened the gate, started to put out a restraining arm, saying, 'You're under arrest...' but he got no further than that. Taylor thumped him in the stomach, then nutted him. The Sergeant was out cold. Taylor went to bed and slept all night and was arrested in the morning. Mellor was taken to the hospital where he remained for a couple of days. Taylor was later discharged with ignominy and sentenced to two years in the 'glass house'.

We were joined in the police section by another acting corporal, a lad called Aaron Cohen, who became one of my best friends. We united because of prejudice, although for me at this camp it was only periodic and mild – but for Aaron it was continual. Being Jewish, he was a prime target for ignorant bigots. He came to the camp upon the demotion of one of the other corporals. The corporal in question was supposed to have been on patrol at Crewe station but it came out at his court-martial that he'd spent most of the time drinking at his girlfriend's flat. In fact when he returned to camp he was so drunk as to be incomprehensible. He was driving an Austin Champ police vehicle and when we tried to pull him out of it with the intention of letting him sober up in one of the cells, he accelerated away fast and finished up inside the fuel store, having knocked down one of the walls. The noise of the collision caused people to rush out to see what had happened, including some of the officers, who issued instructions for his arrest. At his trial later he was sentenced to 112 days' detention, was demoted to ACl, lost his job in the police and became an admin orderly, taking the place of Taylor (who had recently been discharged).

There was a clique of three who barracked and tormented Aaron cruelly. Their favourite saying was, 'Oy Vey, if you vant to buy a vatch, buy a vatch, but if you don't vant to buy a vatch, keep your snotty nose off the vindow.' The ragging was merciless. He could have physically destroyed them: he was very powerful and an expert at self-defence and an excellent weightlifter, but he chose to ignore them – well, he did for six months or so, after which the tormenting stopped. Aaron was a quiet chap, but this particular morning he was unusually quiet and I couldn't help noticing that his hands were bruised and swollen. I didn't ask and he didn't say. When I saw the three troublemakers, things fell into place. They were a mess. Not a word was said – no one asked questions – but the Sergeant patted Aaron on the back and said, 'About bloody time. Looks as if they got what they deserved.' Aaron neither confirmed nor denied his involvement.

It was coming up the anniversary of Sylvy's death and I couldn't get her out of my thoughts. Booze didn't help and

God knows I drank enough. On one occasion I was so drunk I couldn't walk and fell down in the street. Aaron couldn't get a taxi: due to the state I was in no one would take us to the camp. Aaron was worried I would be arrested for being drunk and incapable and lose my career with the RAFP. Not that I had any memory of it, but a young lady who ran a Sunday evening chapel meeting came to our rescue. She took us right up to the gates in her little car and Aaron and the duty corporal got me to the police billet and put me to bed.

The following Sunday I made a point of going back to the meeting rooms to say thank you to our good Samaritan. I sat at the back until the meeting had finished then, somewhat embarrassed, went and thanked her for her kindness. She was so lovely I couldn't take my eyes off her. She said Aaron had told her all about Sylvy while she was driving the two of us back and how sorry she was and any time I felt like talking she would gladly listen. I took her up on her offer and over a period of time we developed a good relationship as I told her about my life before I joined the RAF. I found out she was twenty seven, her name was Daisy, she was a school teacher, originally from a village near Manchester where her father – a clergyman – and her mother still lived and she was engaged to be married to one of the officers from our camp.

One evening after we'd had another of our talks, I invited her to have a drink with me. At first she refused but I said I wanted to say 'thank you' for helping me over a difficult time. We popped into a restaurant, had a drink and then I persuaded her to have a meal. She was laughing at one of my stories about my family when her fiancé walked in. When he saw us his face turned thunderous. As he came towards us I stood up and said, 'Good evening, Sir' which he totally ignored.

Daisy said, 'Hello Ralph, I wasn't expecting to see you.'

'That's obvious,' he snapped.

She took no notice and continued. 'This is...'

Before she could say anything else he again snapped, 'I know who he is and what he is, thank you.'

I didn't like the 'what he is' but as I didn't want to upset Daisy I bit my lip and merely said, 'I'll leave you two alone,' and walked out. As I looked back I could see they were arguing.

I phoned her at her cottage the next evening to say sorry for causing her to have a disagreement with her boyfriend. She said I was to forget it and if I still wanted to buy her a meal she would gladly accept. I realised she was getting back at her jealous fiancé but I wasn't going to miss a chance to take her out. We had a great meal – paid for by some of the money Dad had given me when I went to Cardington – and we flirted with each other. She leant over and said, 'I hope they don't think I'm your mother.' I countered somewhat ungallantly with, 'I hope they don't think you're my Grandmother' (she was a few years older than me). On hearing this, she threw up her hands in mock horror and said, 'You cheeky little monkey!' and we both laughed, enjoying each other's company. Outside the restaurant she offered to pay for her share of the meal. I placed my fingers over her lips and told her I was a secret millionaire and then told her about Dad's gift. Whilst I had my fingers over her mouth she gently bit my fingers and the feelings I had went from the soles of my feet to the top of my head. I hadn't had a feeling like that since 'I had the sun on my back and Sylvy lay in the shade'.

We walked back to her car and drove in silence. I was expecting to go back to the camp but instead Daisy pulled up at a large grassy area near a small pond surrounded by trees. It was a bright moonlit night but as we walked up the lane there was a shower of light rain and I saw one of the most beautiful sights I've ever seen: a rainbow at night time. We watched entranced. As we looked at this wonderful sight we both turned towards each other and lovingly kissed. We returned to her cottage and went to bed. In the morning it was obvious there was no need for me 'to cut my toe'.

I had to be on duty at six o'clock so Daisy drove me only part of the way back to the camp (so she wouldn't be seen) and I ran the rest of the way – to be greeted at the gate by the duty corporal saying, 'Christ, you must have had a good night. You don't smell of booze so you must have been in somebody else's pit, you dirty little bugger.' I smiled and said nothing, had a shower and went on duty. All I could think of was Daisy and all I wanted to do was to be with her.

She broke off her engagement and we spent as much time as we could together. Her ex-fiancé tried hard to get back with her, trying all ways he could think of, but to no avail.

I'd just returned to the camp after spending the morning with Daisy when I was met by the duty officer – who happened to be Ralph Channon – to be told that, with immediate effect, I had been posted. The driver had all the details and they had taken the liberty of packing my belongings. Obviously it was a fix, particularly the twist of their making sure it was Ralph who told me. I felt sick and very angry at the way I'd been treated. It took all my self-control not to knock the smug, gloating, self-satisfied look off his face.

Within minutes I was on my way. The driver was under strict instructions not to stop anywhere – two five-pound notes changed his mind. Daisy was teaching in school so I

told the headteacher it was a family emergency and Daisy
came out of her classroom to speak to me. She was terribly
upset when I told her what had happened. I said that I would
phone her and then we could decide what to do. We cuddled
each other and I left her in floods of tears.

I'd been seconded to a camp near Blackpool in
Lancashire. On arrival, I reported to the Provost Sergeant
who took me in to see a Flight Lieutenant. He told me to
stand at ease whilst he read the papers that had been sent
with the driver. He looked up and said, 'Do you know what
these say about you?'

'No, Sir.'

'Well, it ain't very good and if you're guilty of half the
things said here I can't understand why you haven't been
dismissed.' He looked over his glasses at me.

'Am I allowed to know what it says, Sir?' I asked.

'No, not really. Perhaps you'd care to tell me why you
think you've been sent up here?'

I told him all about Daisy, Flying Officer Ralph Channon
and myself, leaving very little out, including the fact that
Channon was the one who had told me I was leaving.

'Okay, I'll ask you some questions and I advise you to
answer them honestly because you'll be found out if you lie. I
might as well tell you now, you'll be under scrutiny,' the Flight
Lieutenant said. He asked me if I was extremely bad-tempered
and aggressive. Had I assaulted several people? Had I got an
alcohol problem? Was I generally insubordinate and untidy?

To all these I answered a categorical 'No, Sir'.

'I didn't expect you to say yes. To be quite honest, I've
never seen such an appalling record. I'll keep an open mind
and I'll assess you in a few weeks' time.' He paused and then
said, 'I've come up through the ranks and I know that once

you've upset the "Officers' Club" they can make your life hell, so tread carefully.' With that I was dismissed and shown to my hut.

Daisy gave in her notice at the school and drove up at weekends, stayed in a hotel and looked for a flat, eventually finding a suitable one over a shop not too far from the camp. For a few months everything was blissful. We enjoyed the brashness and noise of Blackpool; there was also lovely countryside just a few miles away where we went for walks and had pub lunches. Until she could find suitable employment she helped the elderly couple who ran the shop beneath the flat. After a while, though, I couldn't understand her mood changes – she'd never been like this before.

Things came to a head when I had four days off. I'd arranged to hire a big car and I was going to take her wherever she wanted to go. When I told her she said that she didn't want to go. I rounded on her and nastily snapped, 'What the hell's the matter with you? Nothing I seem to do is right. There's no pleasing you.' I was about to carry on when she stopped me dead in my tracks by shouting at me, 'I'm having a baby,' and bursting into tears. After a while everything calmed down and we discussed what to do next. We decided on a registry office wedding, the two of us and the witnesses, nice and quiet, no fuss, then present the families with a fait accompli. It didn't work out that way. For a few weeks Daisy seemed uneasy and withdrawn. When asked, she said, 'It's probably the baby,' which I accepted.

I called into the florist's, bought a big bunch of flowers and went to the flat, only to find the door locked. The elderly couple came out of the shop and said, 'Daisy's gone away for a few days and asked us to give you this.' They gave me a letter and whilst I was reading it the old man continued, 'There was two men, an older man who was a vicar – I think he was her dad – and a younger man who drove her car away. She got into the vicar's car.' The younger man was Ralph from the description.

I returned to the base in a state of shock. In the letter it said Daisy wasn't coming back and she no longer wished to marry me, but that she was keeping the baby and had the full support of her family. There was a telephone number for me to ring so that a meeting could be arranged to have a full discussion. Everything was so formal. I couldn't believe it was happening. My love for little Sylvy came flooding back, but I was determined to face up to things and not 'go inside myself' again. I sat watching the sun go down over the sea, closed my eyes and concentrated on trying to contact Gran. I felt she was in a bad mood but two hours later I heard Gran's voice in my head say tersely, 'It's the best thing.' That's all she said. I took some leave and rented Daisy's old flat over the shop and hired a car. I arranged to drive over to the village where Daisy's parents lived. Everything was very civilised: I was greeted at the door by her father, taken into the drawing room and provided with a cup of tea (how English!). I was introduced to another man who was the family solicitor – there purely to settle any disputes. I asked to see Daisy and her Dad said, 'You will, it's only right that you should.'

He explained that Daisy had telephoned him to ask his advice, she had told him everything. He knew virtually every detail of our relationship. He also knew all about my family – where we lived, how we lived, he knew all about us. He'd obviously engaged an agent to find out the information. He said, 'The baby is a big factor and she assures me it's yours as you're the only man she has ever made love to. But place that on one side for a moment: please consider the age difference, the big gulf in upbringing and style of life you are both used to. With all due respect to you – and I emphasise I do respect your way of life – can you honestly believe Daisy would settle to living a nomadic life, travelling in a horse-drawn wagon or a caravan. And would she be totally accepted and respected? I'm not being disrespectful to your ladies but they have been born to that sort of life, they are hardy and used to the hardships and rigours of such a life. Daisy wouldn't last. I only want the best for my daughter.'

'So do I,' I replied. 'We would live in a house and she would have all the comforts, if not more than she enjoys now. I need to see her. I'll explain everything, then she can make her decision. I'm as concerned for Daisy and our child as you are.'

The solicitor interrupted us to say, 'You do realise that as the father of an illegitimate child you have no rights whatsoever over that child?'

I didn't answer, saying only that I wanted to see Daisy on her own. The two men left and Daisy came in and sat down opposite me. At first there was an awkward silence, then I told her all about the plans I had, just as I had told her father. I asked her if she loved me to which she said, 'Yes, but do *you* really love me?' Before I could answer she asked me a question that shocked and upset me, 'Because if you do, why do you constantly call me Sylvy when my name is Daisy? You're still in love with the little girl you told me about when we first met. I can't and will not live with that.'

'I didn't know I did that. I'm sorry, I wouldn't deliberately upset you like that. Why didn't you say something to me?'

'I was hoping you would stop. I realised you didn't know you were doing it. I can't marry you. I want to but I'm not going to. I can't compete with a ghost.'

I couldn't answer straight away, I didn't know what to say. We talked for a long while. I tried to change her mind by promising to be a good husband and dad but she was adamant – and later on I had to admit to myself she was right. As I got up to go I said I would contribute to the upkeep of the baby and would keep in regular contact. She said 'No' to both. She wanted a clean break. And then she delivered a bombshell by saying, 'Ralph, despite everything, still wants to marry me after the baby is born and wants to adopt the baby.'

We sat down again and talked for still longer but she wouldn't change her mind, saying it was best for all concerned. I left feeling very sad and rejected and I thought of Gran's words about having had my heart broken once already. She had told me to beware of non-Gypsy girls and find a Romany lass if I wanted to be happy.

I went back to see Daisy several more times but she wouldn't change her mind. As I was leaving after one of these visits, her Dad politely said, 'Please don't come again – you will not be welcome.'

Daisy gave birth to a baby girl in August 1956 and she was christened Fiona Elizabeth. In the following October she married Ralph, who later adopted my daughter. They were posted to Germany and then I lost touch.

By the end of my service I was a Senior Aircraftsman Acting Corporal and was told that if I signed on for another five years I would immediately be promoted to the substantive rank with a very good chance of being made a sergeant within two years. I thought carefully and in the end decided to join the civilian police.

Judging by the sore heads and less-than-sunny dispositions the next day, my demob party was a success. I'd treated my closest friends to a dinner at a local pub then it was open house for anybody from the RAF camp. The large room I'd booked was full to overflowing, money had been left over the bar and jugs of ale were being passed round. On my last leave I had brought back two dozen bottles of homemade plum brandy and the landlord 'closed an eye' when these were put on the tables. The juke box was blasting out all the latest rock and roll music and dancing started when a lot of local girls joined us and couples spilled out onto the street and into the square.

No one took any notice when the town policeman put in an appearance. He was taken by the arm and ushered into the bar and a couple of pints were thrust into his hands which he quickly drank and looked round for more. We found out a few days later he had had a major rollicking from the sergeant as he had been seen injudiciously rocking and rolling with a pretty little girl. It had been a good night. Some of the lads slept it off on the park benches, others who couldn't get all the way back to the camp slept contentedly on the side of the road, one of them was found sleeping up a tree – how he managed to get up it let alone stay up there was a mystery.

After my demob I went back to see the family. When I arrived home at the camp everyone was pleased to see me. The first person I went to see was Gran who said, 'I knew you were coming today. I saw you in the crystal ball, and then I saw you going away again and disappearing into a mist.' As usual she wouldn't say anything else so I spent a lot of time with her telling her about my experiences in the RAF until she dropped off to sleep.

As soon as I saw Dad he started to tell me about all the plans he had made for my future. He was expecting me to pick up where I had left off and become a *groimengro* (horse dealer) like him. The problem was he hadn't asked me. I decided to say nothing until I thought the time was right. Strange how there never seems to be a right time. We were in the field grooming the horses when I said, 'Dad, I'm going to join the police.' I didn't get a chance to say anything else. He dropped his curry comb and advanced towards me with a drained face and wide staring eyes. 'I hope to God you're fooling around again. Cos there ain't any way I'm going to allow you to be a bloody *gavver*. I'm your father and the *Sherengro* and you'll do as I say or you'll be off the camp.' He'd made two mistakes: he'd ordered me to do something and he'd issued a threat. I was accepting neither; I turned and walked away. I hitched a trailer to one of Dad's vans, drove out of the camp and found a parking place a little way from the camp where I spent a restless night mulling over the happenings.

I returned the van and trailer next morning. By then both of us had calmed down and we sat by the river and talked things over. The upshot being he accepted that my mind was made up and he asked me to say nothing to anyone else until I had been accepted into the police. As he pointed out, it would split the family and I would be a *choroid* (outcast).

I applied and got interviews with several forces but, despite my exemplary record in the RAFP, as soon as they heard I was from a travelling family the shutters came down. When I asked why I had been rejected the answer was always 'We're not obliged to give any reason'. I became very disillusioned and was thinking about going back into the RAF when life turned up a coincidence. Eating fish and chips out of newspaper, I came across an article about a Midlands police force that was finding it difficult to get recruits and had reduced their height limit from five foot ten to five foot eight. I wrote giving brief details of myself and was invited for an interview. I was expecting another rebuff.

I sat up in front of the chief inspector who was very impressed with my RAFP record. When they asked me for details about myself (which would be verified later) I had to tell him about my background. His face fell and he said, 'Oh Jesus! This could be a problem not only for us but for you as well. Stay there, I'll be back in a few minutes.' Not long after he came back and said, 'I've seen the Chief Constable and discussed everything with him and his words were that he doesn't care if you're striped like a humbug – if I think you can do the job then I'm to take you on, subject to our normal checks. Also you're asked not to let anybody else know about your connection to the Travellers, okay?' I agreed. He then told me I would be receiving an official letter giving all the details of the training course and the starting date of my employment as a police officer. I couldn't stop grinning to myself.

Now I had to face my Dad and the rest of the family. I felt sorry for Dad when I told him I had been accepted and he asked me if I still thought I had made the right decision. He wanted to know about the wages and when I said it was nine pounds two shillings a week he couldn't believe it.

'Is that all? How the hell are you going to live on that? If you stay with me we can be partners and I can more or less guarantee you'll get at least two to three thousand pounds in a year, not a paltry four hundred. Think about it before you commit yourself.'

The money was tempting but I still needed to get away so I said to him, 'I'm sorry, it's what I want to do and I want your blessing.'

He could see I wouldn't change my mind. He replied, 'I think you're making a big mistake. I'm not going to fall out with you or argue any more. You must do what you want to do, so long as you realise it will be hard to come back, if not impossible.'

I said that I was leaving on Saturday and he asked me not to say anything to the others until the Friday evening. Then he asked me if I would go into town with him the following morning but not to ask why. So I said I would.

Next morning we parked the lorry and walked down the high street. Passing a car showroom I spotted a Zephyr – a Mark 1 Zodiac – on display. I put my nose against the window and said to Dad, 'Look at that, isn't she beautiful?'

'I expect you'd like to own one of those, wouldn't you?'

'You never know, dreams come true sometimes' I said back to him.

'Well, that car is yours. It was going to be a "Welcome Home" present. Now you can have it as a farewell gift.' At this point Dad looked crestfallen and I felt so sorry for him, but I'd made my decision.

'Are you sure? Do you really mean it?'

'Yes, I do. Son, I love you, I don't agree with what you're doing, in fact I'm dead-set against it, but all I want is for you to be happy again. When you leave us I need to know we're still good friends. I don't want to lose my son altogether.'

We went inside. The car was ready to drive away. Everything had been pre-arranged by Dad. I couldn't believe it. A Ford Zephyr Zodiac, two-tone colour – dark blue and cream – whitewall tyres, heater, spot lights, radio and leather trim and it was mine (I found out later it had cost Dad around £900). I drove out of the showroom and went for a spin. I felt like a king. I pulled up in a quiet spot, looked at Dad and said, 'Sorry I've upset you.'

Before I could say anything further he held up his hand for me to stop talking. 'I've decided to let your cousin Kezz come into partnership with me, so don't get worrying, just make sure you're successful. Let that be an end to it now.' Then he said, 'We've one more thing to do'. He told me to drive to the bank in town, which we did. The local priest, Father Bartholomew, had made the necessary arrangements on Dad's behalf for me to have a bank account and all I needed to do was sign the forms. The manager greeted us like long-lost friends and took us into his office where everything was explained to me and the forms signed. Dad had put money into a deposit and current account for me (he told me later that for the three years I had been away he had put thirty pounds on one side each week as if it had been my wages). It had been to give me a good start in his business – there was five hundred pounds in one account and four thousand in the other. It would've taken me ten years to earn that sort of money. Although things had worked out badly for Dad, he said the money was still mine.

When the rest of my relations found out about my plan to join the police there was uproar. I was told, 'If you show your back to us, we will show our backs to you. You will be banished.'

The evening before I left I said my goodbyes to Dad and went to see Gran, who was surprisingly calm and said very little about me becoming a *gavver*. She had a twinkle in her eye when she gave me a big tub of hedgehog grease, saying, '*Gavvers* spend a lot of time on their feet: use this grease every day on them. If you don't look after your feet you won't be able to do your job properly.' And that's all she said about the police. I cuddled her and kissed her and said I would come back and see her, to which she said, 'I've told them before, if they try to stop you coming to my funeral I'll come back and haunt them and they're afeared of *bavolengroes* (ghosts).' She cackled to herself. 'You go now, I'm tired. I'll be watching you.' With that she snuggled down and went to sleep. I kissed her forehead and left.

The next morning I put what belongings I had into the boot of my new car. There was an eerie silence over the whole of the camp, no noise, nothing, not even a dog barking or a baby crying, nothing. I drove out in silence. One life had ended, another had begun. A whole new world awaited.